How to Make Yourself Happy and Remarkably Less Disturbable

How to Make Yourself Happy

and Remarkably
Less Disturbable

Albert Ellis, Ph.D.

Impact   Publishers, Inc.
Atascadero, California 93423

Impact Publishers and colophon are registered trademarks of
Impact Publishers, Inc.

ATTENTION ORGANIZATIONS AND CORPORATIONS:
This book is available at quantity discounts on bulk purchases for educational, business, or sales promotional use. For further information, please contact Impact Publishers, P.O. Box 6016, Atascadero, California 93423-6016 (Phone: 1-800-246-7228).

Library of Congress Cataloging-in-Publication Data

Ellis, Albert.
    How to make yourself happy and remarkably less disturbable /
Albert Ellis.
        p.   cm.
    Includes bibliographical references and index
    ISBN 1-886230-18-8 (pbk. : alk. paper)
    1. Anger. 2. Rational-emotive psychotherapy.   I. Title.
BF575.A5E444   1999
158.1--dc21   99-12793
                                                               CIP

Publisher's Note
This publication is designed to provide accurate and authoritative information in regard to the subject matter covered. It is sold with the understanding that the publisher is not engaged in rendering psychological, medical, or other professional services. If expert assistance or counseling is needed, the services of a competent professional should be sought.

Cover design by Foster & Foster, Inc., Fairfield, Iowa
Printed in the United States of America on acid-free paper
Published by **Impact ☙ Publishers**®
POST OFFICE BOX 6016
ATASCADERO, CALIFORNIA 93423-6016
www.impactpublishers.com

Contents

Acknowledgments

I would like to thank several of my associates who read and commented upon this book when it was still in manuscript — notably, Shawn Blau, Ted Crawford, Raymond DiGiuseppe, Dominic DiMattia, Kevin Everett FitzMaurice, Steven Nielsen, Philip Tate, Emmett Velten, and Paul Woods. I greatly appreciate their helpful suggestions.

I would also like to thank Tim Runion, who saw the manuscript through several word processing revisions and Ginamarie Zampano, the administrative director of the Albert Ellis Institute, who facilitated the gathering of some of the material and the working out of many administrative functions in regard to getting it ready and who did so in her usual most competent manner.

Finally, let me express my gratitude to Bob Alberti, the remarkably energetic editor of Impact Publishers, who not only did the usual kind of careful editing of this book but also made some unusually creative suggestions for additions to it.

For Janet L. Wolfe

*My loving mate, fine collaborator, and indispensable partner
in running the Institute for 34 memorable years.*

On Making Yourself Happy and Remarkably Less Disturbable

When I first saw Rosalind, she was severely depressed. Her husband had recently divorced her, and she cried and lambasted herself for being "a failure." She was anxious about doing poorly at work — although she was talented and successful as a clothes designer — and she put herself down for being anxious and depressed. She had a neurotic symptom about her neurotic symptoms!

She had been telling herself about her job, "Yes, I do some fairly good designing for my firm, but I'm not half as good as I *should* be. It's just a matter of time before they discover this, see how poor a designer I really am, and sensibly fire me." This created her anxiety.

I first helped Rosalind to stop calling herself "a failure" and to accept herself *with* her depression and anxiety. Yes, I agreed, she could be a *person who* failed — but not "a failure." (A genuine failure, after all, could only and always fail and would be undeserving of succeeding.) Like the rest of us humans, she was too complex — with so many "good" and many "poor" traits — to be given one global, total rating.

At first, Rosalind resisted my attempts to persuade her to stop rating her *total self*, her whole *being*. "After all," she countered, "*I* am responsible for my foolish acts with my ex-husband and I am depressing and panicking myself. Since *I* am the one who does poorly, why shouldn't I rate *myself* as a failure?"

I disagreed. True, Rosalind at times failed — but she also often succeeded. She did poorly — but she also did well. "You're responsible for all the *good* things you do, such as successfully designing clothes. Does that make you a *good person*? No, you are simply a *person who* acts well and badly; and you are a *person who* has millions of thoughts, feelings, and actions. Those, too, are good, bad, and neutral. Why, then, rate *yourself* as bad for your bad *behaviors*?"

Rosalind finally got my point, and began to stop damning her *self*, her *being*, for her failing *actions*. She first accepted herself *with* her disturbances. Then, to her surprise, she saw that her original depression about being rejected by her husband and her anxiety about failing at her job both virtually disappeared. After accepting herself *with* her disturbances, she quickly gave up her demands that she *had to be* a perfect wife and designer.

When Rosalind adopted the REBT philosophy of rating only her *actions* and not her *self*, she greatly changed. She concluded, "*Nothing* can really make *me* bad — no matter how I *behave*. I'd better behave competently and lovingly, for that will improve my work, my relationships, and my other pleasures. That would be great, but I don't *have to* be achieving and lovable to be an okay human."

I saw Rosalind for just a few months and was amazed at her progress. She not only made herself undepressed and unanxious but she also remained healthy. She referred several of her close friends and relatives to me, and almost all of them reported how much she had improved and how much she kept improving. From time to time she also attended my famous "Friday Night Workshop" at the Albert Ellis Institute for Rational Emotive Behavior Therapy in New York, where I regularly give live public demonstrations of REBT with volunteers from the audience. She spoke briefly to me at these workshops and showed continued progress and much greater happiness.

Rosalind's case was one of hundreds that showed me that REBT can help people:
- make profound philosophical changes,
- reduce their presenting symptoms,
- tackle other emotional problems,
- rarely fall back to old disturbances, and effectively use REBT methods whenever they do upset themselves again.

How Did She Do It?

Rosalind first used REBT's method of *unconditional self-acceptance* (USA) to stop denouncing herself about her primary symptoms: depression and anxiety. Second, she saw that these symptoms themselves stemmed from damning herself for failing in her marriage and for possibly failing on her job. When she gave up self-blaming, she no longer felt depressed and anxious.

Rosalind went further. She looked at some of her other anxieties — especially her fear of public speaking — and saw that they, too, largely followed from blaming herself when other people criticized her. And she used REBT to become able to risk speaking in public and to accept herself unconditionally, even when she was anxious and — most importantly — even when she gave a poor speech!

Next, Rosalind rarely fell back to being depressed about her divorce and panicked about her job, and when she did fall back, she did so only fleetingly. Finally, when she was depressed, anxious, or otherwise disturbed about anything, she assumed that she had again begun to *musturbate* (which I'll explain later) again, figured out her foolish demandingness, quickly disputed it, and once again felt unupset and happier.

Rosalind's progress showed me that many REBT users could improve *elegantly* — that is, first overcome their presenting disturbances and then proceed to use REBT methods to make themselves remarkably less disturb*able*. Since the 1950s I have seen and/or heard from hundreds of my clients and readers who were able to do this.

Readers, Too?

Yes, readers. Here is a recent case. Mike, a 38-year-old computer consultant visited me from Wyoming a few weeks ago. Raised in New York, he had all his life been panicked and obsessive-compulsive about doing anything imperfectly — even "poorly" playing the piano for pleasure. He moved to Wyoming because New York, with its complicated living conditions, was "too dangerous." He reported that years of psychoanalysis hadn't helped him at all; but that a year of cognitive-behavior therapy in Wyoming helped a little, so that he cut down his OCD (obsessive-compulsive disorder) somewhat and lived more comfortably with it.

Six months before he came to see me in New York — mainly to thank me — Mike started reading *A Guide To Rational Living* and several of my other books. For the first time in his life, he began to fully accept himself *with* his panic and his OCD and he immediately felt and acted much better. His panic-about-being-

panicked completely vanished. His original panic states —
mainly about failing in sexual intercourse with women — were
greatly reduced. His OCD diminished. Whenever he fell back to
any of his old disturbances he quickly accepted himself *with*
their reappearance and soon overcame them again. When he
visited old friends in New York and they acted childishly, he
refused to horrify himself about this — as he had previously
always done — and he actually helped them by teaching them
some of the principles of REBT.

Mike remarked during his first and only session with me, "I
won't say that I am an entirely new man from reading your books.
But almost! Practically none of the things that I used to panic
myself about are upsetting today. And when I at times return to
my old perfectionism, I quickly find my *shoulds* and *musts*, kick
the hell out of them again, and go right back to leading a
productive and enjoyable life. As I said before, I mainly revisited
New York to meet you personally and to thank you for all you've
given me. Your books are miraculous — although I don't really
believe in miracles. Thank you, indeed, for writing them!"

Can You Really Change Yourself?

Rosalind and Mike, along with many other individuals who had
REBT sessions or who read my writings, have convinced me that
people *can* deeply, intensively, and "elegantly" change their
disturbances and their disturb*ability.* Do they completely
change their "personalities" if they use REBT? No, not exactly.
A "personality" includes several strong biological tendencies —
such as introversion or extraversion. You can change these
tendencies somewhat by working very hard. But not completely.
So, for the most part, you'd better accept your basic
"personality" and live with it.

Even your tendency to disturb yourself is partly innate.
As an individual person, you may have natural, inborn
tendencies to make yourself anxious (overconcerned), to be
depressed (horrified about unfortunate events), or to be self-
hating (damning your entire *self* for some of your poor
behaviors). If you have these inborn tendencies, you do not have
to *go along with* or *give into* them. That's right. *Inborn* doesn't
mean *fixed.* For example, even if you are born with poor musical
abilities, you can get musical training and you can improve them
somewhat, though not completely. If you naturally hate spinach,
you may train yourself to enjoy it *somewhat*.

Yes, you can change your disturbances, too. Even if you are born and raised to be "easily upsettable," you can largely change this and make yourself much less so. How? By working to use several of the REBT methods I will describe in this book.

Fortunately, you *choose* to indulge in your emotional problems. Your biology and your upbringing may indeed *encourage* your doing so. But you still have considerable ability to stop your neurotic tendencies in their tracks and to reduce them.

Take my own case, for example. I seem to have been born with a sweet tooth, as was my mother. She indulged in all kinds of sweets until the age of 93, when she was caught stealing candy from other residents in her nursing home! Up to the age of 40 I followed Mother's example — took four spoons of sugar and half a cup of cream in my coffee, ate a pint of ice cream every day, fried my macaroni in butter and sugar, and continually indulged in my favorite drink: a chocolate or malted milkshake. Great stuff!

At 40, however, I became diabetic. So I immediately — the first day I found that I had diabetes — stopped eating sugar, ice cream, milkshakes, butter, and other fatty foods. Do I miss them, 46 years later? Yes! Do I indulge in them? Just about never.

So even if you are born with a strong tendency to act self-defeatingly — as I believe billions of people are — you can definitely change it. You can train yourself to behave for your own interest, and for the interests of the social group in which you choose to live. When you behave neurotically, you create problems within yourself (intrapersonal problems) and problems with and for others (interpersonal and social difficulties). So you'd better work to improve both these areas. Books and cassettes on REBT show you how, as do many other cognitive-behavioral self-help materials.

So *use* these materials. Learn how to change your thoughts, feelings, and actions and thereby reduce your emotional distress. Keep reading and using the procedures in this book to help yourself. If you work at it, you will most probably have some real success in undisturbing yourself, and relating better to others.

Why Another Self-Help Book?

You may wonder why I have written this additional book, when I have already published 40 other self-help volumes — as well as hundreds of articles and audio-visual cassettes — to show people how to deal with their personality problems?

For a special reason. In 1996 I published a book for mental health professionals: *Better, Deeper, and More Enduring Brief Therapy*. It presents the general principles of Rational Emotive Behavior Therapy but is my only book — and one of the few in the entire field of psychotherapy — that specifically tells therapists first, how to help their clients *generally* improve; *and*, second, how to *elegantly* change. It emphasizes what my previous books on REBT only lightly describe: How to help people make themselves not only less disturbed but less disturb*able*.

I am quite pleased with *Better, Deeper and More Enduring Brief Therapy*, and expect it to help many therapists and their clients. While writing it, however, I realized that these clients could well use self-help materials, in addition to those that I and other REBTers have published, that would show them how to work with their therapists. And also, how to work by themselves to achieve *elegant* change. Yes, *elegant*.

More precisely: I wrote the present book to show you, its reader, several important aspects of emotional change. Through reading it, you will see how:

- You may needlessly and foolishly go along with your inherited and acquired tendencies to make yourself severely anxious, depressed, enraged, self-hating, and/or self-pitying.
- You can change your thoughts, feelings, and actions that lead to your disturbances and thereby make yourself considerably less upset and less self-defeating.
- You can persistently and strongly use — and keep using — REBT methods until you automatically and habitually follow them, and thereby make yourself less disturbable even when Adversities occur — or you make them occur — in your life.

You can use this book to make yourself less neurotic and less disturbable, by learning and practicing the following:

- To a large extent, you disturb yourself. You don't merely get upset by present or past situations.
- Because you largely choose to upset yourself, you can therefore choose to unupset yourself.

- You mainly choose to upset yourself by creating absolutistic musts and demands — by taking your healthy
  preferences for success, approval, and pleasure, and
  turning them into unhealthy, insistences and commands.

As you clearly see these tendencies to disturb yourself, you
can go on to the following practices:

- Persistently change your tyrannical musts to strong
  flexible preferences.
- Forcefully change the disturbed feelings and actions
  that accompany your musts.
- Make yourself think, feel and act in non-demanding
  ways.
- Acquire a steady, strong philosophy that helps you to
  believe that nothing — yes, nothing — is awful, horrible, or terrible, no matter how bad, inconvenient, and
  unfair it may actually be.
- Stop damning yourself and others by fully accepting
  the view that wrong, unethical, and foolish acts never
  can make you or them into bad or rotten people.
- Acquire the self-helping philosophies that are later
  described in this book — especially the philosophy
  that no matter what losses, frustrations, failures, and
  handicaps, occur (or you make occur!), you still have
  the ability to create for yourself a reasonably productive and happy life — though perhaps not as happy as
  you could have without these difficulties.

How Can You Make Yourself Happy?

Can you really achieve the increased happiness and freedom
from disturbance that I have just outlined? Yes, most probably
you can — if you work at following the suggestions in this book.
Why? Because you, being human, are *born* with constructive
and creative tendencies, and you are also born with the ability to
sharpen and increase these self-fulfilling tendencies.

As Jean Piaget, George Kelly, Michael Mahoney, and other
psychologists have shown, humans, you and others, are born
with a strong tendency to deal *constructively* with the many
problems you face during your early and later life. If not, you
would not eat proper food, would not figure out how to get safely
through heavy traffic, and would allow yourself to be continually
exploited and victimized by unethical people. So you cautiously

face thousands of problems, figure out how to solve them — and keep yourself alive to face still more problems. We humans are inborn constructivists! We — and that includes you! — actively and spontaneously strive to solve life problems. You *naturally* observe difficulties — and more-or-less solve them. Otherwise, you would be *kaput!* Dead as a duck — and at an early age!

You not only act constructively when confronted with physical problems — eating, drinking, walking, and whatnot — you also are mentally and emotionally inventive. When you feel quite anxious, depressed, or enraged, you *notice* your feelings, rate them as "good" or "bad," and often do your best to change them for "better" ones. This is because your basic goals are to remain alive and be reasonably happy. Whatever discomfort, pain, or unhappiness you experience — whether it be physical or mental — you observe, think about it, and push yourself to reduce it. That, again, is your creative nature. So use it!

Unfortunately, we humans also have an innate, biologically inclined, *destructive* nature. Many Pollyannaish and "spiritual" books on reducing your misery fail to tell you that part! Of course, you rarely deliberately sabotage yourself. Nor do you consciously create needless emotional and physical misery. You *can,* but you rarely do. You're not *that* crazy! Instead, you are born with the tendency to think, feel, and act easily and often in ways that are self-defeating and socially-sabotaging. Yes — easily! Yes — often! And you add to your inborn destructive tendencies by adopting more of them from your parents and culture. So you are doubly unblessed!

Take procrastination, for example. You are given a task to do — at school, at work, or in your family — and you see that you will get good results (like approval and self-satisfaction) if you do it. So you agree to take it on.

But, but, but! — you foolishly delay, you put it off and again and again. Why? Because you (stupidly!) *think,* "I'll do it later. It will be better and easier if I do it later." Or you *think* (idiotically!), "I *have* to do it perfectly or else I'm a no good, and inadequate *person!* So I'll do it later." Or you *think* (asininely!), "They *should not* have assigned this difficult task to me. They are unfair! It's not only hard but also *too hard* for me to do. To hell with them! I'll do it when I *feel like* doing it. Or maybe I won't do it at all! I'll show them!"

If you are a "normal" person, you *easily* and *strongly* create excuses and self-defeating thoughts like these. And, along with them, you create unhealthy negative, *feelings* — like anxiety and hostility — as well as procrastinating *acts* — like delay, sloppy performances, or complete inertia. Also, once you procrastinate, and once you realize that you'll never get what you want that way, you frequently *think*, "I'm *a no good person* for procrastinating! I'm *unable* to finish this task on time. People will despise me for delaying. And they're right — I *am* a worthless idiot!" These thoughts *about* your procrastination are partly designed to move your butt and get you going. Actually, though, they help you believe that *you*, your *whole personhood*, are no good. Then, because a no-goodnik like you presumably *can't* do well, your self-downing thoughts encourage you to procrastinate more!

Procrastination, moreover, is often naturally self-reinforcing. If you are a talented perfectionist, you may make yourself so anxious about doing a job imperfectly that by putting it off you reduce your anxiety and — temporarily! — make yourself feel *good*. Paul Woods, a well-known REBT practitioner, calls this kind of anxiety reduction *relief*. You then feel so good that this "reward" helps you, again, procrastinate even more!

Nobody's Perfect, But...

Procrastination is only one of the many examples I shall give in this book to show that, along with your healthy, excellent tendencies to be constructive and creative, to be nicely self-helping, you *also* have unhealthy, destructive tendencies to needlessly harm yourself. Your self-defeating tendencies, moreover, are usually powerful and frequent. So if you are wise, you will use your healthy, constructive urges — and you will minimize your unhealthy ones now *and* in the future.

That is the main purpose of this book: to show you precisely what your natural constructive tendencies are and how to push yourself to *use* them to overcome your harmful leanings.

Permanently, perfectly, for all time and under all conditions? Obviously, no. Because of your biological and social nature, you will remain a distinctly *fallible* human. We all do. None of us — you included — is perfect or superhuman. We and you — everyone, all of us — frequently do self-sabotaging things. And we shall continue to do so!

This book, then, will show you how to make yourself *much less* disturbed than you often do. Uniquely, it will try to teach you how to *un*create your emotional and behavioral problems —

and how to *keep* them minimal: to make yourself, as I said before, considerably less disturb*able* about past, present, and future Adversities. Finally, when you do, as you sometimes will, fall back to occasionally upsetting yourself again, it will show you how to quickly and determinedly *unupset* yourself. Doing so, you then can tend to make yourself still *less* disturbable.

Really? Yes, *really* — if you read on and *if* you PYA — push your ass — to *use* some of Rational Emotive Behavior Therapy (REBT) methods in this volume. No miracles — as many "New Age" treatises cavalierly promise you. But, with hard work and practice, you *can* make yourself distinctly less upsettable. Yes, you *can.*

What's Really Different About REBT?

Why is this book rare among the tens of thousands of self-help books, pamphlets, and articles that have been published for many years? After all, most self-help books help you *feel* better, and that is what you want. This book goes beyond that. It helps you *get* better — to function more effectively and happily. And it helps you *stay* better — to refuse to upset yourself in the future.

The methods in this book that help you feel better, get better, and stay better might just turn out to be the most important information you've ever learned. This approach has brought important relief from misery to many of my clients and to thousands more who have read my books and listened to my cassettes. Interestingly, I discovered them not only from the practices I learned as a psychologist, but also from the writings of philosophers.

At the age of 16, I studied philosophy as a hobby, long before I even thought of becoming a psychotherapist. I was particularly interested in the philosophy of human happiness. So I started devising ways for people — notably myself! — to reduce their emotional upsets and increase their sense of fulfillment in life.

When I used these sensible philosophies in my own life, I rarely felt miserable about anything. And when I started doing therapy in 1943, I began teaching my clients some of the wisdom I had learned. Unfortunately, I sidetracked myself in 1947, when I began training in psychoanalysis and began practicing analytic therapy for the next six years. I foolishly bought what most therapists were then selling and thought psychoanalysis was "deeper" and "better" than other forms of psychological treatment. But my experience in using it with my clients taught me — to my surprise — that it obsesses about people's early histories and ignores the *beliefs* people use to seriously upset themselves about their life events. And with psychoanalysis, I wasn't nearly as effective as I had been prior to using this method.

Back to the drawing board! At age 40, I returned to the studies I had started as a teenager — this time not as a hobby, but to develop a theory to help people manage their emotional problems. I went back to several ancient philosophers including the Asians, Confucius, Gautama Buddha, and Lao-Tsu; and the Greeks and Romans, especially Epicurus, Epictetus, and Marcus Aurelius. I also re-read several modern philosophers, such as Spinoza, Kant, Dewey, Santayana, and Russell, to see what they said about misery and happiness. They said quite a lot!

On the basis of some of these philosophies, I founded Rational Emotive Behavior Therapy (REBT) in January 1955. This is the first of the cognitive-behavior therapies that focuses on thinking, feelings, and actions as the main sources of your "emotional" disturbances, and that emphasizes changing your attitudes to reduce your disturbed emotions and behaviors.

I wanted REBT to work quickly and efficiently, and I soon saw that it did. I discovered this myself during my first year of using REBT, and I published a study showing that it was more effective than the classical psychoanalysis and analytically-oriented psychotherapy that I used from 1947 to 1953. Since then, a large number of research studies have shown that it and the other cognitive-behavioral therapies that followed it are unusually effective — often in a brief period of time.

2

Discovering, Disputing, and Demolishing Your Disturbing Demands

Let us suppose that when you upset yourself — feel and act against your own interest — you turn your healthy *preferences* into unhealthy, irrational *demands* and *musts*. As I will explain and emphasize throughout this book, *you can quickly find these Irrational Beliefs and Dispute them.*

As a simple rule for finding your irrational beliefs, assume that just about all your dogmatic musts fall under three major headings. Here are three main musts to look for when you bring on disturbed feelings:

Feelings of serious depression, anxiety, panic, self-downing: "I *absolutely must* perform well on important projects and be approved by significant people or else I am an inadequate and unlovable person!"

Feelings of strong and persistent anger, rage, fury, impatience, bitterness: "Other people, particularly those I have cared for and treated well, *absolutely must* treat me kindly and fairly, or else they are rotten individuals who deserve to suffer!"

Feelings of low frustration tolerance, depression, self-pity: "The conditions under which I live *absolutely ought to be* easy, unfrustrating and enjoyable or else the world's an awful place, I *can't stand* it, and I'll never be able to be happy!"

If you have any of these disturbed feelings, and if you act against your own and your social group's interest, look in your heart for these major musts. Assume that you have one, two, or all three of them, and that you are a talented human who *easily* manufactures these demands, and then just as easily attaches them to Adversities in your life.

Why do you so often "musturbate"? Because, like other humans, you are often naturally grandiose. Once you are born, get to be a few years old, and have the strong desire to remain alive and happy, you *easily* create demandingness. You *often* jump from, "I really *want* to succeed" to "I absolutely *have to!*" From, "I truly *hope* that you like me" to "Therefore, you absolutely *must!*" From, "I *wish* my living conditions were comfortable" to "Consequently, they *have got to* be!"

Do you always turn your strong wishes into arrogant commands? No, not always — but often! If your moderate desires — like winning at ping pong or seeing a movie — are thwarted, you can live without greatly upsetting yourself. Sometimes! But if you have strong, powerful urges — like being a ping pong *champion* or seeing your favorite star in the outstanding movie of the year *tonight* — watch it! Just let *this* urge be thwarted and you'll often scream like a banshee: "I *must* not be deprived. How *awful.* This makes me furious! I *can't stand* it! My life is empty. What's the use of going on?"

Were you *born* demanding? Probably yes. As an infant, you *needed* to be cared for, fed, kept warm, and be protected from harm. Otherwise, you were a goner — wouldn't survive to demand and to complain today.

In addition, to being born needy, you were often *spoiled rotten* as a child — given many of the things you wanted, without having to work hard to get them. You were probably loved and adored just because you were young and cute. And you perhaps were pampered by parents and relatives who were egotistically delighted to have you as *their* child, grandchild, niece, or nephew.

Later on, things got no better in regard to your childish demands. Your culture loudly told you — with fables, stories, movies, TV commercials, and popular songs — that you *should* have expensive toys, indulge in all the ice cream you could eat, be the smartest and most talented kid on the block, and get everything you really wanted. Still later, these same mass media often insisted that you absolutely *should* be a rock star, make a million dollars, and be President of the United States. Yes, at the very least! Actually, these media tell you that it is highly *preferable* for you to perform well. But you often *interpret* this as a *demand.*

Your grandiose tendencies, as you can see, are both born and bred. You *naturally* make your strong desires and preferences into arrant and arrogant demands. For you *not* to do so would take a good deal of time and effort — which you rarely bother to take!

But let's face it — you'd better! As an adult, you can certainly live with your childish expectations and demandingness. If you are like most of us humans, they won't kill you. But they will often make you miserable. Yes, almost inevitably.

Why? Because your musts are contradicted by social reality. Personally, you *can't* always succeed — not to mention succeed perfectly. Being a fallible human, you just can't.

As far as your demanding that other people *must* incessantly please you, love you, and do your bidding — forget it! They simply won't. Believe it or not, they are mainly absorbed in pleasing themselves — beasts that they are!

As for world conditions being arranged so that they *have to* give you exactly what you want the moment you want it — alas, no! Not a chance. Frankly, the universe doesn't give a hoot for your desires, and has no personal interest in you. No, none whatsoever. The cosmos doesn't love you or hate you — it just spins along its merry — and its unmerry! — way. The people who live, as you do, in this world presumably could change many of its conditions. Yes, they could do something about economics, politics, the ecology, and other harsh situations. But will they? Not very much! Not very thoroughly! Not very often!

There we have it. You want, greatly want, to do well, to be treated kindly by others, and to have comfortable living conditions. Fine — go ahead and want. But when you think you've *got* to have, when you *demand*, the fulfillment of any of these desires, take care! Your godlike commands will often lead to disillusionment, frustration, and "horror." Not that you, others, or world conditions will truly *be* "horrible." But once your holy musts are not fulfilled, you will easily *see* conditions as "horrors" and make yourself unduly upset.

That's what your dogmatic, absolutistic musts create — *awfulizing, I can't-stand-it-itis,* and *damnation* of yourself and others. These follow from your musts, and often become Irrational Beliefs in their own right. Thus, when you tell yourself the three crazy musts mentioned above, you often add several secondary Irrational Beliefs:

- "Because I *absolutely must* succeed in my relationships (or in sports, or business, or art, or science), and I'm not succeeding as well as I *have to,* (1) It's *awful* and *terrible!,* (2) I *can't stand* it!, and (3) I'm a *worthless, undeserving person!*"

- "Because you don't treat me as kindly and fairly as you *absolutely should*, (1) It's *awful* and *terrible*!, (2) I *can't stand* it!, and (3) You're a *worthless, undeserving person!*"
- "Because my living conditions are uncomfortable and frustrating, as they *absolutely ought not* be, (1) It's *awful* and *terrible*!, (2) I *can't stand* it!, and (3) The world's a rotten place that will *never* give me what I really want and deserves to go up in smoke!"

Again, you are born to be easily disturbable. You are also bred to expect to attain what you strongly want. And your culture often teaches you that you *deserve* fulfillment. But you'd better not continue your childish demands. Using REBT, you can actively Dispute the Irrational Beliefs that block you from thriving in this frustrating world.

What can you do to reduce your powerful musts and their self-sabotaging results? Well, when you feel and act destructively, you can find your musts, then Dispute them, and change them back to preferences or Effective New Philosophies. You can also Dispute your awfulizing, I-can't-stand-it-itis, and damnation of yourself, of others, and of the world. For instance, you can use these realistic, logical, and practical Disputes:

- *Disputing Awfulizing:* "Why is it *awful* and *terrible* if I don't succeed well or if people and conditions I encounter treat me badly?"

First Answer: "It isn't! If it were *awful* it would presumably be as bad as it could possibly be, or *100% bad*. Obviously, however, it could be *worse* than it is. I could fail even *more* than I am now failing and people and conditions could afflict me *more* than they are now afflicting me. Virtually nothing that I can encounter is *totally* or *100% bad*."

Second Answer: "When I view it as *awful* and *terrible*, I often imply that it is *more than* bad, or *101%* bad. But *nothing* can be *more than* 100% bad."

Third Answer: "If it were *awful* and *horrible*, it would be badder than it *absolutely should* be. But it is just as bad as it now *is*. In fact, it *must* be just as bad as it now *is*. It can't, right now, be *less* bad than it is. But since my calling it *awful* means that I consider it *so* bad that it shouldn't exist, and since everything that exists *has* to exist, nothing is really *awful, terrible*, or *horrible* — all of which words really mean extreme badness. Many things are *bad* or *very bad* — that is, against my interests and against the interests of the social group in which I choose to live. But, however bad they are, they can only be *highly unfortunate* and/or *very inconvenient*. Never *awful, terrible,* or *horrible* — except by my arbitrary, self-defeating definition. Only damned bad! So let me do my best to change this unfortunate condition — or accept it and live with it if I truly find that I can't change it. Whining about how *awful* it is will only make it seem worse than bad — and make me feel *more* miserable!"

Fourth Answer: "If I define failure and rejection as *awful* instead of as *bad* and *unfortunate*, what will this definition get me? Usually, quite *awful* results! I'll tend to hate myself, other people, and the world, and make myself more miserable than I otherwise would be. Deep depression is what it often will get me."

- *Disputing I-Can't-Stand-It-Itis*: "Where is the evidence that I *can't stand* very uncomfortable, frustrating, and unfair conditions?"

Answer: "Nowhere! — I'm just inventing it. If I *really* couldn't stand such bad conditions, I would die because of them. But I'll rarely die of discomfort, frustration, or unfairness — though I could foolishly kill myself because I *think* I can't stand them.

"Again, if I *really* couldn't stand losing a loved one, failing at a job, or being treated unjustly, I then could not be happy *at all*, could not enjoy *anything* for the rest of my days. Hogwash! No matter what conditions exist in my life — yes, even poverty or fatal illness — I can *still* find *some* enjoyable pursuits — if I *think* I can and if I try to find them! So I *can* stand, *can* tolerate, almost anything that I really don't like."

- *Disputing Damnation of Yourself and Others*: "In what way am I a *worthless, inadequate person* if I don't succeed as well as I *must*? How do other people become *no good*, become *undeserving people*, if they don't treat me as well as *they absolutely should?*"

Answer: "In no way whatsoever! I may often do foolish, stupid *things*, but my incompetent *acts* never make me a *worthless, inadequate person*. Unless I *define* myself that way! Other people may easily treat me badly and unfairly but their poor *behavior* never makes them *bad, undeserving persons*. No human, including myself and others, is subhuman — at worst, is only *a highly fallible, unangelic person*.

Disputing your self-defeating, Irrational Beliefs is one of the main and most helpful methods of REBT. You can honestly acknowledge that other people and things practically never seriously upset you but that you, instead, can choose or *not* choose to agonize *about* the unfortunate Activating Events or Adversities that they may put in your life. You can use this effective key to *Stubbornly Refuse To Make Yourself Miserable About Anything* — *Yes, Anything!* — as I say in the title of one of my most popular REBT self-help books.

Really? Yes, really. You may be born and reared with a strong tendency to make yourself panicked, depressed, or enraged about many things — as, alas, many people are. And, because these disturbed feelings also have biological aspects, your brain and body chemistry may catapult you into a state of emotional disturbance when few or no Adversities are occurring in your life. Too bad! Tough! You may, without your own crazy ideas, be practically *thrown into* feeling and behaving dysfunctionally. Yes, from your biological tendencies and — sometimes — from unusual handicaps you suffered, such as, malnutrition or physical abuse. Nonetheless, the feelings of horror and the terror that you now experience *about* these emotional and physical handicaps are still largely your own doing — the result of your thinking.

How so? Because even when your biology and your history encourage disturbance, you "normally" have a strong tendency to upset yourself *about* this upsetness. Thus, your biochemistry may be out of whack and you may wake one morning seriously depressed for no special reason, then perhaps stay depressed until your chemical imbalance rights itself or you help it do so with antidepressants. But to *add* to your depression, you often may tell yourself, "I *must* not be depressed!" "It's unfair that my biochemistry is off, and I *can't stand* this unfairness!" "What a worthless person I am for becoming depressed — especially when I have no good reason for feeling this way!" These Irrational Beliefs *about* depression will magnify and multiply natural unpleasantness — and often make you much more depressed than you were at first.

Similarly you may have been practically driven into a depressed state as a child by serious physical or sexual abuse that you could not defend yourself against. But not completely: If 100 other children were just as sorely abused as you were, hardly all of them would seriously depress themselves.

Anyway, if you are *still* very upset about being abused as a child, you are now, probably, irrationally thinking, "My early abuse *absolutely should not* have occurred!" "Such unfairness is *awful* and I *can't* stand even thinking about it now!" "The people who abused me are completely rotten! I'm going to spend the rest of my life hating them and getting even with them, if it's the last thing I do!" "I must have been a weakling to let myself be abused!" These Irrational Beliefs will keep your original upsetness vividly alive — instead of letting it die a natural death, as disturbance gradually does if you don't dwell on it and reinforce it by continual crooked thinking.

Moral: Even when biochemical handicaps and abusive traumatic experiences easily get you going on the way to severe panic, depression, and rage, your self-sabotaging, irrational thinking also may contribute to your emotional woe, may keep it alive, and may greatly intensify it. So take responsibility for at least *some* of your acute and prolonged upsets. And be glad that you are responsible. As I keep noting, you are *lucky* that you yourself help to create and perpetuate your disturbances. For that means that you personally can *stop* them in their tracks. Yes, you can! — if you take your personal power and use it.

Are you also lucky if you are a "nice neurotic" who experiences the usual frustrations and Adversities of life — such as failing in school, in a job, or in love — and who musts and demands and consequently over-reacts emotionally? Is this better than having a biochemical imbalance that helps you have a severe personality disorder?

Frankly, it is. What I call nice neurotics — or almost all the members of the human race — *choose* to over-react to unfortunate Adversities by foolishly insisting that they must not occur. They consciously and unconsciously *train themselves* to do so. Therefore, they can — though with some effort — train themselves to accept, though not to like hassles and difficulties. Fine!

More seriously disturbed individuals can also undo some of their upsetness. But not that easily! And with more — and sometimes much more — time and effort. So let us hope that you, like most people, are a common garden variety neurotic. Then this book is really for you, and can be most helpful in a fairly brief period of time. If, of course, you heed it and use it. That's right — *use* it and *practice* its methods.

But suppose you're worse off — you're somewhat more than neurotic. Shall you then quit reading, see a psychiatrist, rush for medication, perhaps go for a stay in a mental hospital?

Not exactly. Some of these procedures may possibly help you. So don't always refuse them or insist that you *absolutely must* conquer your emotional ailments on your own. If you have diabetes or cancer, you see a physician — if you are not a fanatic naturist. If you are mentally ill, you see a mental health professional. Rush, don't walk, to the best available clinic or practitioner. No matter how troubled you are, medication and psychotherapy are almost always available. Seek professional help. Soon!

Will this book still be useful? Most probably, yes. Rational Emotive Behavior Therapy and Cognitive Behavior Therapy, which this book describe, are successfully used with some of the most troubled people, including psychotics and those with severe personality disorders. Although they are not completely cured they often are greatly helped to live more productively and happily. So if you or one of your friends or relatives is mentally ill, careful reading and applying the methods in this book may be quite helpful. Letters from hundreds of my readers and listeners to my cassettes have vouched for this over the years. Numerous mental health professionals have also told me how their patients and clients have often greatly benefited from written and spoken REBT materials.

Back to you. You are reading this book, presumably, because either you or your associates have emotional problems. Will its methods serve as a miraculous cure? No. Will they help considerably? Most likely, yes. *If* you carefully consider and apply them. Try them out. Experiment. See for yourself how they work. If they help you to be somewhat less disturbed and happier, fine. If they help you to make deeper and more enduring improvements in your emotional health, let me know. If they help you to *make yourself happy and remarkably less disturbable, wonderful!* That is my goal for you. I think you *can* achieve it. If you do, let me hear from you. I am compiling a book of reports from people who used REBT and other methods to help themselves significantly change. How about letting me include your story?

The next chapter describes in detail the ABCs of Rational Emotive Behavior Therapy (REBT). You can quickly start using them to reduce almost any emotional disturbance — and then proceed, a little later, to *deep, intensive, more enduring self-therapy.*

3

The ABCs of
Remarkably Changing Yourself

Keep this in mind: You largely *make* yourself disturbed, and you *make* yourself happy.

In my first self-help book, *How To Live With A "Neurotic,"* I showed that emotional disturbance" largely consists of stupid behaviors by non-stupid people. When you are disturbed you set up goals and purposes — especially, to stay alive and be happy — and then you (incredibly!) act against them. By thinking, feeling, and behaving stupidly, you get — no, largely *make* yourself — severely anxious, depressed, enraged, self-hating, and self-pitying. Along with these self-sabotaging feelings, you often under-react (cop out, procrastinate, withdraw, or develop phobias) or over-react (addict yourself to alcohol, drugs, overeating, smoking, or other compulsions).

What a mess! Luckily, however, if you are disturbed, you largely *make* yourself that way — create your self-defeating behaviors. That is one of the main teachings of Rational Emotive Behavior Therapy (REBT), and one that I shall keep demonstrating throughout this book. You do not passively *get* or *become* upset. No, you largely consciously and unconsciously *manufacture* your own disturbances. And, you will see, that's good. Yes! Because if you make yourself upset, you usually have the ability and the power to act less stupidly and to *un*upset yourself.

By following REBT teachings, you have the ability to unupset yourself so often and so strongly that you can actually make yourself, distinctly less upset*table* for the rest of your life. Which means? Which means that if you intelligently think, feel, and act against your own tendencies to create emotional problems for yourself (and others), and if you *keep* doing so, you will rarely seriously disturb yourself about anything (yes, anything). Also when you foolishly fall back to re-upsetting yourself, you can quickly, and sometimes easily, stop doing so by once again using the same techniques you used before. You can do all this when you use the methods of REBT or the somewhat similar methods of other forms of cognitive behavior therapy (CBT), that follow the theory and practice of REBT.

What Exactly Is REBT?

How can you use REBT to quickly make yourself happy and less distressed for the rest of your life? First, let me explain the simple but highly important ABCs of REBT which, when I first developed them in 1955, I built mainly on the work of philosophers, rather than psychologists or other mental health professionals of that time. (Some of the following ideas — minus the ABCs — you encountered in the previous chapter.)

Briefly, you start with Goals (G's) and then you often encounter Activating Events or Adversities (A's) that block or hinder these Goals. Thus:

- *A (Activating Event or Adversity)*. For example, wanting to succeed in a course, at work, at a sport, or in a relationship, and actually failing.
- *B (Beliefs)*, especially *Irrational* Beliefs, about failing and getting rejected. For example, "I *must* not fail! I *have to* get accepted! It's *awful* to fail! I'm *no good* for being rejected!"
- *C (Consequences)* that follow Adversities and Irrational Beliefs. For example, feelings of severe anxiety and depression. Self-defeating behaviors like withdrawing and giving up your Goals. For example, quitting a course, not trying for a good job, withdrawing from participating in a sport, or refusing to date or make close friends.

To illustrate, let us start with C (your emotional Consequence), which usually follows almost immediately after you experience A (unfortunate or undesirable Activating Events or Adversities). Well, no. To be more accurate let us go back a little before A and C to G (your main Goals).

Let us assume that your main Goals (G's) are to remain alive for many more years and to live happily — especially with a long-term partner. Why are these some of your main Goals?

Because you believe they will bring you joy. You have chosen them on the basis of your biological tendencies, your family and cultural experiences, and your personal, individual preferences. Fine. You are entitled to choose these Goals (Gs) — or almost any other Goals — as long as, preferably, you don't interfere with other people choosing and trying to achieve their own personal Goals.

Assume, now, that you are alive and kicking, but that your important Goal of having a long-term relationship is blocked. At point A (Activating Experience or Adversity) the person whom you most desire rejects you as a partner, and says, "Stay out of my life! I have no interest in relating to you. You are just not my type!"

Well! Your A is opposed to your Goals and interests, and is therefore quite unfortunate. A real bummer. So at point C (your emotional Consequence) you almost immediately feel bad. To say the least, you feel frustrated and disappointed, because your Goals, your legitimate preferences, are now blocked, thwarted, dashed. That's hardly "good" or "great." Not to you!

REBT holds that when you feel frustrated and disappointed (at C) after your Goals are blocked at A (Adversity) your feelings are negative *but* are healthy and useful. For when a potential partner rejects you, it will hardly be good or healthy if you make yourself feel happy or elated. You then will *like* what you did not *want* to occur. How odd and unhealthy that would be!

Also, after you are rejected at point A (Adversity) it is hardly good if you feel totally indifferent or neutral at point C (Consequences). Because you will then tend to give up your Goal of involving yourself in a long-term relationship and will not try to relate to another partner.

The A-leading-to-C connection of REBT says, therefore, that when any of your Goals (G's) are blocked by Activating Events or Adversities (A's) you had better have fairly strong negative feelings or emotional Consequences (C's). Otherwise you will not motivate yourself to look for and try to arrange better, less unfortunate Activating Experiences (A's) that will help you, sooner or later, to fulfill some of your fondest Goals.

Fine. But the A-leading-to-C connection of REBT says that you had better *not* create *unhealthy* or *disturbed* negative feelings at point C (Consequences) after you experience unfortunate A's (Activating Events). These *unhealthy* Cs are feelings like severe anxiety, depression, self-hatred, rage at others, and self-pity. Why had you best avoid experiencing these C's

(Consequences)? Because they usually interfere with your fulfilling your Goals, and they also tend to feel unnecessarily painful in their own right.

The A-to-C connection also warns you against creating self-defeating *behavioral* C's, which frequently accompany your unhealthy *emotional* C's. Thus, if you feel severely depressed (C) after a potential partner has clearly rejected you (A), you may also, at point C, act shyly when you meet other potential partners, or you may refuse to date anyone. This prevents you from being rejected and from making yourself depressed again. Or, going to the other extreme, you may compulsively date a great many potential partners in your desperation to win at least one of them.

REBT makes this unusual point: You can *choose* your emotions and behaviors. When your important Goals are blocked by Adversities you can largely *choose* to have either healthy or unhealthy feelings at C (Consequences) and you can also *choose* to act either helpfully or defeatingly at C. Almost always, you *will* react at C after you experience an unfortunate A that blocks your desires and Goals (Gs). But *how* you react is largely up to you.

Here we come to the B's in the ABCs of REBT. B is your Belief System — what you think, imagine, and evaluate about A. First, B includes preferences, wishes, and wants; and, second, absolutistic demands, commands, musts, shoulds, and oughts. So your B's include Beliefs that are widely different and that may lead to healthy *and* unhealthy C's.

Take your preferences first. Your important reasonable Goal, again, is to relate intimately with a steady partner. At A (Activating Event or Adversity) you are rejected by the main potential partner you select, who says, "Stay out of my life! I have no interest in relating to you. You're just not my type!" End of potential relationship.

Suppose, now that your main Belief (B) about this rejection (A) is *only* a *preference* or a *wish*: "I really *wish* I had been accepted by this potential partner and strongly *prefer* not being rejected. *But* I have other choices. I can find another suitable mate and enjoy myself in a new relationship. Even if I *never* relate steadily with a chosen partner, I can still live and be happy with short-lived relationships — or even be happy alone. Okay, now how do I still find the kind of mate that I prefer?"

When you really hold *preferential* Beliefs at point B in your ABCs, how will you feel when Adversity strikes at point A? Answer: Very likely, quite *sad* and *disappointed.* These are *healthy* feelings because you are not getting what you really *want* and these negative feelings will motivate you to keep trying to get it. That is good. Negative feelings like sadness, disappointment, regret, and frustration *spur* you, and the rest of the human race, to push yourself to *change* unfortunate A's and to *produce* more fortunate ones, such as subsequent acceptance and mating. So they are negative but still *beneficial* feelings. You *healthily* create them when your wishes are frustrated. So keep making your Beliefs (B's) *preferential!* They give you helpful feelings.

Watch out, however, if you hold *demanding* or *commanding* Beliefs (B's) about your unfortunate A's (Adversities). Suppose you get rejected by a potentially "good" partner, and you Believe, "I *absolutely must not* get rejected! I *have* to get accepted! I *need* a steady partnership and losing this one *proves* I am a worthless person! This rejection is *awful!* I can't stand it! I might as well quit trying to relate." How will you *then* feel at point C (Consequence)?

Most likely, depressed, panicked, and self-hating. And where will your demanding Beliefs (B's) and unhealthy feelings (C's) get you? Probably nowhere. They will encourage you to withdraw from dating, and to give up trying to mate. Or to settle for a partner for whom you don't really care. Not very healthy behaviors!

To summarize: When your important Goals are blocked by Adversities (at point A) and you mainly *prefer* and *wish* (at point B) to get what you want and to keep seeking it if you can't achieve it, right now, you will produce healthy negative feelings (emotional C's) that lead to constructive actions (behavioral C's). But if you make your Beliefs (B's) into absolutistic *musts* and *demands*, you will often produce unhealthy, destructive negative feelings (C's) that will lead to self-defeating actions (C's). You start by creating an A-to-C connection, but really your B-to-C connection is more important, because what you think, imagine, and conclude about A, at point B, largely *creates* the kind of feelings and behaviors you produce at C.

If the ABCs of REBT are accurate — and many psychological experiments and psychotherapy and counseling sessions tend to show that they are — you, as a thinking human, have the ability to observe your Beliefs, to see how your absolutistic *demands* and *musts* mainly *create* your destructive feelings and behaviors, and to change them back into strong *preferences* instead of grandiose, unrealistic *commands*.

For example, suppose your Goal of mating is thwarted by the

Adversity (A) of being rejected by a "great" potential partner, and you feel depressed and worthless (emotional C's) and you stop trying to look for a partner (behavioral C). Feeling and acting so bad, you want to change your C's to healthy ones. How do you arrange to do this?

Mainly by proceeding to D (Disputing). You acknowledge your destructive B's — which in REBT we often call Irrational Beliefs (IB's) — and you challenge and Dispute them (D) until you make them into healthy Rational Beliefs (RB's) or preferences. You do this in three major ways: by making yourself *think, feel,* and *act* differently.

It's the Thought That Counts

Let's see what you can do by thinking differently. Knowing that you are feeling and acting destructively (against your Goals and interests), you *assume* that you have healthy preferences (RB's) *and* unhealthy musts and demands (IB's). You figure out and find the latter. You come up with the IB's mentioned before: "I *absolutely must not* get rejected! I *have to* be accepted! I *need* a steady partnership and losing this one *proves* I am a worthless person! This rejection is *awful!* I *can't stand* it! I might as well quit trying to relate."

You then Dispute (D) these Irrational Beliefs (IB's) in three main ways: (1) Realistically or Empirically; (2) Logically; and (3) Practically. Doing so, you come up with E — an Effective New Philosophy.

Let's try some of this Disputing.

1. *Realistic or Empirical Disputing.* "Where is the evidence that I *absolutely must not* get rejected?" *Answer (E, Effective New Philosophy):* "Nowhere — except in my nutty head! If any law of the universe said that I always *have to* be accepted, I would have been! Obviously no such law exists. The fact is I *was* rejected, and may well be in the future. Now what can I do to get rejected *less* often and accepted *more* often by people I would like to relate to? I *prefer* being accepted but I clearly don't *have to* be."

2. *Logical Disputing.* "I very much *want* a steady partnership, but how does it follow that I *absolutely need* one? How does losing this possible partner *prove* I am a *worthless person? Answer (E, Effective New Philosophy):* "It doesn't. It only proves that I failed this time but not that I am a Failure, with a capital F, whose inner essence is worthless. I can't logically jump from 'I *performed poorly this time*' to 'I *am* a poor, lowly *person.*'"

3. *Pragmatic or Practical Disputing.* "If I keep believing, 'I *absolutely must not* be rejected,' 'I am a *worthless person* if I am not accepted,' 'This rejection is awful,' and 'I can't stand it!' where will these Irrational Beliefs (IB's) get me?" *Answer (E, Effective New Philosophy)*: "Nowhere. I'll make myself feel very depressed. I'll believe that I can't be accepted by a good partner — and that belief will help me keep failing. I'll make myself withdraw from trying to get a partner and therefore may never get one. If I finally win a good mate I'll still be so anxious about later losing my partner that I may easily ruin the relationship!"

When you keep actively and persistently Disputing (D) your self-defeating, Irrational Beliefs (IB's), you will probably soon come up with alternative preferential Rational Beliefs (RB's), such as: "I hate being rejected by this potential partner, *but* I can find one who accepts me and, if not, still lead a happy life. It would be great if I were accepted, *but* I never *have to* be. I want what I want, *but* I don't *absolutely need* it! I failed this time, *but* I am never a total Failure. This rejection is highly *inconvenient*, *but* not *awful* or *terrible*! I'll never *like* being rejected, but I *can* stand it and still lead an enjoyable existence."

If, after any important Adversity (A) occurs, you feel and act self-destructively, if you assume you have absolutistic, necessitous demands and musts (IB's), and if you forcefully keep Disputing these IB's, you will often wind up with preferential Rational Beliefs (RB's) that will lead to healthy feelings and actions. And you will probably fulfill more of your Goals and get fewer frustrations and annoyances.

So active, vigorous, persistent Disputing of your self-sabotaging Beliefs can help you immensely. It leads to healthy thoughts, emotions, and actions. What else works? Many other thinking, feeling, and behavioral methods. As I have noted in my books for professionals and public readers, REBT is always pluralistic or multimodal. I shall go through the best of its methods in later chapters of this book.

dispute a history —

4

You Can Change If You Think You Can
Five Self-Starting Beliefs

For thousands of years philosophers and preachers have said and written: You *can* help yourself with your emotional problems. The ancient Asians, for example: Confucius, Gautama Buddha, Lao-Tsu, and many others. The ancient Greeks and Romans: Zeno of Citium, Epicurus, Cicero, Seneca, Epictetus, Marcus Aurelius, and others. The early Jews and Christians: Moses, the writers of Proverbs, Talmudic commentators, Jesus, Paul, and others.

The view that you can help yourself largely continued in more modern times in the work of many writers and philosophers. For example: Maimonides, Spinoza, Kant, Emerson, Thoreau, Dewey, and Russell. Unfortunately, this view was sabotaged by Sigmund Freud and many other therapists who agreed that the "right" way to help yourself is by taking a talking cure with a sympathetic professional. Alfred Adler, Carl Jung, Erich Fromm, Karen Horney, and Carl Rogers, among many other therapists, largely upheld this position. Most therapists still do. If you feel anxious, depressed, or enraged, most of them say, you had better get months or years of talk therapy to let go of your disturbance.

Well and good. But these professionals don't go far enough. I have been a hard-working psychotherapist for over 55 years, and have had more sessions with more clients than perhaps any other therapist. At the age of 85, I still mainly see clients from 9:30 a.m. to 11:00 p.m., including leading four therapy groups each week, and conducting my regular Friday Night Workshop, where I have public sessions with volunteer clients. So I am not exactly lazy!

In the beginning of 1955, I helped change the face of psychotherapy by starting the first of the cognitive behavior therapies, Rational Emotive Behavior Therapy (REBT). This is one of the main talking therapies, because I speak with my clients and they usually talk very freely to me. It is also a relationship therapy. As an REBTer, I always do my best to unconditionally accept my clients, whether or not they act well or are lovable. I also teach them how to unconditionally, under all conditions and at all times, accept and forgive themselves — though not, of course, many of the things they do. In addition, REBT includes social and interpersonal skill training.

Right from the start, it has also pushed homework assignments, including reading, writing, listening to recordings, attending lectures and workshops. I wrote my first book on REBT, *How To Live With A "Neurotic"*, in 1956 and soon followed it with a number of other books for the public on personal functioning and on sex, love, and marriage relationships. Some of these — such as *A Guide To Rational Living* — were so successful that they encouraged a number of other authors to write cognitive behavioral self-help books. Look at the *New York Times* and other lists of non-fiction best-sellers, and you will usually find some of these near the top of the list.

The main point of these self-help manuals and of the present book is simple: You *can* distinctly help yourself with your emotional problems. Where shall you start? Being a philosopher as well as a therapist, I say: With several constructive attitudes. You can change if you *think* you can. Let us consider, in this chapter, several crucial self-changing thoughts.

First Self-Starting Belief:

"Because I Am Mainly A Self-Disturber, I Can Definitely Stop Disturbing Myself."

As I observed in the previous chapters, psychoanalysis and most other forms of psychotherapy tell you that your parents, your culture, and your godawful past make you disturbed. Nonsense! These situations often do you little good and much harm. So they *contribute to*, but hardly *cause* your disturbance. Oddly enough, *you* do. You are born and reared with a talent to enjoy yourself — *and* to upset yourself.

When you do yourself in, you also have a tendency to deny this and to blame your self-defeating feelings and actions on others: *"You* made me angry." *"My partner* upset me!" *"The weather* depressed me." *"The situation* caused me to feel anxious."

False. But this way of copping out is wrongly invented by almost everyone and has been upheld over the centuries by countless psychologists, writers, poets, historians, and sociologists.

Why do we tend to make this wrong conclusion? Because we naturally think this way. Even the most intelligent of us frequently survey our lives and come up with this "fact." We are born and reared to be highly suggestible. And we often have difficulty looking at what we call reality, accepting many of its grim aspects, and taking responsibility for many of the bad things that happen to us. We prefer to blame other people and events for these happenings; and although we are partly right about this, we are also often self-deluded.

Take a common happening in your early childhood. You accidentally spill a glass of milk while you are eating, you and the table get wet, and you are yelled at. You feel upset and start to cry. Then you are yelled at for crying, perhaps get hit by your parents. Then you feel more upset and have trouble calming down, even though your family members try to help you do so.

When you view these incidents as a child, you see that you spilled the milk and that several "bad" things happened right after that. You therefore rightly connect the two: first, the Activating Event or Adversity (A), the spilling of the milk; and second, the Consequences (C's) of your parents yelling, your upset feelings about this, your being hit for being upset, your being upset about being hit, and your having trouble calming down. However, you may wrongly believe that you caused all these Consequences to happen.

In the course of your observing this "natural" chain of events, you may see the Activating Event (A), the spilling of the milk, as "bad" or "unfortunate," because it leads to such unpleasant results. Actually, it is neither good nor bad, because *some* children and their families may look at it and define it — at point B — as good and pleasant, and may think it great that you, the child, is having such a good time eating, playing with the glass of milk, and learning how to cope with this "interesting" situation. They may then — at point C — laugh about it.

Many other families, however, may look at this same Activating Event (A) as an "awful" Adversity. Because they see (or define) your spilling the milk — at point B — as "terribly bad," they may yell at you — at point C — for being "naughty," for "stupidly" upsetting yourself, and for "foolishly" continuing to feel upset when they are trying to calm you down.

In other words, the Consequences (C's) that follow your accidentally spilling the glass of milk (A) definitely are not merely *caused* or *determined* by what happened (A). In this case (and in innumerable other cases) C clearly follows or "results" from A, but C is not truly *caused* by A. As emphasized in Chapters 2 and 3, C is also *created* by B, the Beliefs that your parents, your other family members, and you yourself have *about* A.

This is what continually happens to you as a child, as well as in your later life. Activating Events (A's) are made "good" or are "bad" even though they are not in themselves that way. Your Beliefs (B's) about your A's depend upon many factors that lead you and other people to view the A's of your life as "good" or "bad."

Thus, if your parents are tolerant and tend to view most of the things you do (A's) — including spilling milk — as "good," you tend to view these A's that way yourself. And if they view your (A's) as "bad," you tend to view them that way, too. You then tend to forget that it is your and their Beliefs that make your milk-spilling A's "good" or "bad."

If you clearly and strongly acknowledge that you mainly upset yourself about Adversities (A's), you also have a key to not doing so. Don't think that you can wholly change you or your entire personality. You have strong biological and social tendencies to be the way you are. In addition, you have *practiced* doing "good" things and "bad" things for many years. So don't think that you're going to change yourself completely. Remarkable changes in yourself you can make — with persistent effort and practice. But not complete, not perfect, not absolute. Be persistent, be determined. But don't believe that you *must* become perfect!

Discover what works for you. No plans, including those outlined in this book, work for everyone. Try what you think will work, acknowledge when it does — and when it doesn't. When it doesn't, consider alternative paths. If you have trouble changing yourself, find a good therapist to work with. When you are seriously disturbed, you may have special physical and emotional deficiencies. Your neurotransmitters in your brain may be working defectively. Your chemistry may be out of balance. By all means try self-help methods and psychotherapy first. But don't reject possible medication. It may help immensely.

Experiment. See what works for you. Watch out for the gurus and the other crackpots who claim miracle cures. Seek counsel with trained professional and not with New Age or Old Age quacks. When anyone offers you a quick, miracle cure and has no scientific data to back it up, run, run, run to the nearest and best professional you can find.

Let's get back to your attitudes, especially those toward self-change. The Little Engine That Could *thought* it could run. First of all, then, you'd better strongly think, believe, and — yes! — *feel* that you can control your own emotional destiny. Not others' thoughts and actions. No. Not the fate of the world. No. But *your* thoughts, feelings, and actions. Yes! Here, in this chapter, let me present some more starters.

Second Self-Starting Belief:

"I Definitely Can Reduce My Irrational Thinking That Sparks My Emotional And Behavioral Problems."

As I have been noting in the first three chapters, you largely are able to *choose* whether to disturb or not to upset yourself about undesirable happenings. You often can't control the Activating Events or Adversities (A's) that happen to you but you have a great deal of control over your Beliefs (B's) *about* these A's. You therefore can control your emotional Consequences (C's) that largely follow from your Bs.

When undesirable A's occur, you can helpfully tell yourself, at point B, "I don't like this undesirable A, so let me see if I can change it or remove it. But if I can't change it, too bad. I'll put up with it for the present and gracefully lump what I can't change. Later, I'll see if I can't improve it."

Thus, if you fail in business, in a relationship, or in a sport (at point A) you can convince yourself (at point B) that you don't like failing, but it's not your last chance, it's not the end of the world, and that failing doesn't make you a total Failure with a capital F. You will then (at point C) feel sorry and disappointed, which are healthy negative feelings, but will not make yourself horrified and depressed, which are unhealthy and self-defeating feelings.

But suppose, on the other hand, you experience the same kind of failure (at point A) and you strongly believe (at point B), "I *absolutely must never* fail! It's *awful* and *horrible* when I do! Failing makes me a totally incompetent person!" You *then* create the Consequence (C) of making yourself feel anxious, depressed, or self-hating and frequently also *create* destructive behaviors, such as avoidances, addictions, and compulsions.

REBT, then, urges you to accept responsibility, not for most of the undesirable things that happen to you (A's) but for your Beliefs (B's) about these A's. It shows you how to preserve your Beliefs as preferences — "I would like A to be better than it is, but if it is unpleasant I'll somehow deal with it and not demand that it *has to be* better to make my life satisfactory. I'll either change A or somehow enjoy myself in spite of it." If you stick with such *preferences*, you will then feel sorry or frustrated when you don't get what you want. These negative feelings are healthy because they encourage you to change undesirable Adversities (A's) — or to live with them without unduly disturbing yourself *about* them.

REBT also says that when you demand that unfortunate A's *absolutely must* not be as bad as they actually *are*, you create disturbed, dysfunctional feelings and behaviors. Thus, when you strongly Believe (at point B), "I *absolutely must not* lose so-and-so's approval!" you will make yourself feel unhealthily depressed (rather than healthily disappointed) when you do lose it. Even when you do gain his or her approval, you will make yourself panicked about whether or not you will *later* lose it! So your raising your *desire* to a *dire necessity* almost always does you in. And you thought it was your horrid mother and father who made you so miserable today! Let's face it, *you* did. You accepted their view that you *need* — and not just *want* approval. You still devoutly Believe that you *need* it.

REBT tells you that whenever you think, feel, and act against your own best interests you practically always raise one of your healthy goals or preferences into an absolutistic, rigid *should*, *ought*, or *must*. Why do you often do this? Because you're human, and humans *easily* take their strong desires and make them into grandiose demands.

Very foolish! — backing up your strong desires with absolutistic demands. But that's the way you and other humans often behave — foolishly. And when you don't get anything you think you absolutely must get, you often unrealistically and more foolishly conclude, "It's *awful* (totally bad or more than bad)!" "I *can't bear* it (will die of being deprived)!" "I'm *no good* for not achieving what I really need!" "Now that I've failed to get what I completely must have, I'll *never* be able to get my needs fulfilled!"

Fortunately, you not only largely disturb yourself when you think, feel, and act self-defeatingly, but you are also born and reared with constructive tendencies that you can use to *un*disturb yourself. Although, as noted above, you often cannot change the Adversities (A's) that you dislike, you can almost always importantly change your Beliefs (B's) and feelings (C's) *about* these A's. Why? Because you upset yourself. Therefore you, luckily, can practically always *un*upset the one person in the world whose thoughts and feelings you control — you!

Third Self-Starting Belief:

"Although I Am Distinctly Fallible And Easily Disturbable, I Also Have The Ability To Think, Feel, And Act Differently And Thus To Reduce My Disturbances."

You weren't exactly born disturbed. No, you learned and con-structed self-defeating thoughts, feelings, and actions. You were, however, born with both self-helping and self-defeating *tenden-cies*. Strong tendencies! Too bad. But don't blame yourself for your upbringing nor for your *self*-destructiveness. You naturally, humanly acquired both.

You were particularly born fallible — highly imperfect. No matter how bright and talented you are, you are error-prone, a natural mistake-maker. Because you're human. Because you're alive. You don't have to like this. But you'd darned well better accept it. You *fallibly* do, and will continue to do, many stupid, self-defeating things. Once again — you're human. Not Superman or Wonder Woman. Not a god or goddess. Always fallible. Often very fallible. Whether you like it or not.

Nonetheless, you do have *some* choices. Just because you, like all humans, are *prone* to behave self-defeatingly doesn't mean you *have to* do so. You may be born and reared to easily eat a gallon of ice cream, smoke three packs of cigarettes a day, and enormously clutter your house or apartment. But that doesn't mean that you *must*.

Sure, you don't have *absolute* free will. You are at least partly determined or conditioned by your heredity and your early environment. But not completely! You *can* choose to eat little (or no) ice cream, stop smoking, and keep your house uncluttered. You *can* treat your children nicely even though you may have been abused as a child. You *can* choose to follow any religion (or no religion) you want to follow, no matter what you were taught during your early years.

You *do*, especially, have a choice of what to Believe (B) about the Adversities (A's) that happen to you. Yes, you were born with awfulizing and whining *tendencies*. Yes, your parents, friends, and culture often encouraged you to damn yourself, others, and the world. Yes, you *easily* turn your healthy preferences into self-destructive, absolutistic, grandiose demands. But in spite of your biology, your genes, your family, and your culture you don't *need* to stupidly disturb yourself.

Whatever your nature and your nurture, when you are disturbed, you Believe (at point B, again!) destructive ideas *today*. One of REBT's famous insights says that you largely (not completely) upset yourself as a child by taking your inborn and learned goals, values, standards, and preferences and *raising* them to rigid, unhealthy, musts, shoulds, and oughts. Your parents and culture, no doubt, helped you to do so. But you still *chose* to Believe these absolutistic musts yourself. Yes, *yourself.*

Worse yet — or in some ways best yet — no matter how, when, where, and under what conditions you originally went along with others' irrational Beliefs or invented your own self-defeating IB's you *still*, if you are disturbed, hold on to them *today*. This is another of REBT's most important insights: You *now* Believe that you *absolutely must* do well, that other people *have to* treat you nicely and fairly, and that conditions that you dislike *completely should not* exist. So, whatever happened to you in the past, your *present* IB's upset you. Therefore, you can *now* change them back to healthy *preferences*. You have a *choice*. Make it!

Fourth Self-Starting Belief:

"My Emotional Upsets Include Thoughts, Feelings, And Actions That I Can Observe And Change."

Not completely, of course! You can convince yourself, "I don't *need* good food and can survive when it's rotten." But you'd better not convince yourself, "I can get along well with no food at all!" You can get yourself to Believe, "I don't *absolutely need* a lot of money to be happy." But you'd better not Believe, "I can be deliriously happy even when I am homeless and penniless."

However, because you largely *created* your depressed feelings about someone rejecting you and because you still insist that this person *must* love you, you *can* stop demanding his or her love and thereby *can* stop depressing yourself. Definitely yes, if you are what I call "a nice normal neurotic."

So you *can* change — unless you rigidly *think* you can't. Your "emotional disturbance" usually includes strong feelings — such as panic and depression — but it also includes thoughts and actions. When you *feel* anxious, you usually *believe* anxiety-creating thoughts (for example, "I'm not speaking as well as I *must*, and that's *awful*!) and you *behave* poorly (for example, avoid public speaking). When you think self-defeatingly (for example, "I'm a total idiot!") you feel badly (such as, depressed) and act poorly (such as, avoid schooling). When you behave dysfunctionally (such as, avoid sports), you think irrationally (such as, "I'll always lose and get laughed at") and feel upset (such as, self-hating).

Bullet

Because your disturbances include thoughts, feelings, and actions, all of which tend to be self-destructive, you can make a three-way attack on them: change your thinking, your emoting, and your behaving. That is why REBT is multimodal — why it provides you with *many* methods of modifying your ideas, your feelings, and your behaviors.

Do any of these methods work all the time for all kinds of upsetness? Not by any means! John, Joan, and Jim were all phobic about attending a company party, all of them panicked about going, about socializing poorly, and about being rejected by their co-workers. John convinced himself, "If I go and socialize poorly, too damned bad! I'm still okay!" Joan made herself very anxious by imagining herself doing badly at the party but used Rational Emotive Imagery to make herself feel only sorry and disappointed rather than panicked and depressed. Jim didn't change his panicky thoughts or feelings but made himself go, very uncomfortably, to the party, and spoke to ten different people till he became more comfortable. John, Joan, and Jim, using these different methods, all finally went to the party and enjoyed it. Jane, who was at first more phobic than any of them, went for some REBT sessions, used several different thinking, feeling, and behaving therapy methods, and not only overcame her party-going fears but several of her other disturbances as well. Moral: Convince yourself that several therapy roads work. Use your head, your heart, and your hands and feet!

Fifth Self-Starting Belief:

"Reducing My Upsetness Almost Always Requires Persistent Work And Effort."

This is another famous insight of REBT: You definitely can change most of your self-defeating thoughts, emotions, and actions — but only with much work and practice. Yes, w-o-r-k. Yes, p-r-a-c-t-i-c-e. You'd think that this insight would be pretty obvious. But is it? Not to many therapists who swear by psycho-analysis or New Age cults. But these "magical" helpers forget that first, you (and other humans) are born easily disturbable. Yes, *born.* Secondly, you are often encouraged and conditioned to be upsettable by your nutty parents and culture. Thirdly, you work and practice from early childhood onward to maintain your dis-turbed habitual behaviors. Fourth, you often get help from other irrational friends, fanatical cultists, and even ignorant therapists — who unwisely add to your own destructive thinking. No wonder you require so much work and practice, and then still more effort and practice, to live more healthily.

But face it — you do. There is no magic, no free lunch. Self-change, while almost always possible, requires persistent work and practice. Mainly by following the REBT slogan: PYA — Push Your Ass!

5

On the Road to Less Disturbable

When you behave self-defeatingly — and you often do, human that you are — you are able to discover what you are thinking, feeling, and doing to needlessly upset yourself. You also are able to use Rational Emotive Behavior Therapy (REBT) to *unupset* yourself. If you keep striving to acquire rational, self-helping attitudes, you can actually make yourself much less upsettable. You then only rarely make yourself severely anxious, depressed, enraged, self-hating, and self-pitying. If and when you fall back, you know what to do to reduce these feelings — especially, to change your absolutistic musts and demands into healthy wishes and preferences. You *can* do this!

Great. If you are really determined to make yourself remarkably less disturbable and to become one of those rare humans who consistently copes with Adversities and practically never whines about them, you can follow the principles I previously outlined — and then go several steps further. What are those steps? To steadily practice several *key* philosophies that will help make you considerably less upsettable than the great majority of other people in this difficult world.

Can you really do this? Yes, if you are truly *determined* to make yourself much less upsettable. Yes, if you have what is called — and often wrongly called — will power. Let me show you what this is, and how to get it.

The Power of Will Power

The terms *will* and *will power* may seem similar but actually are different. *Will* mainly means choice or decision. You choose to do (or not to do) this and you decide to do (or not to do) that. As a

human, you obviously have some degree of will, choice, or decision-making. You will, or choose, to buy or not to buy a car. You
may not have the money to buy it or the ability to drive it, but
you can still decide to buy it — and decide to get the money for
it and the skill to drive it. The will to change merely means that
you decide to change — and then (perhaps!) work at doing so.
Will power, however, is more complicated and different. When
you have *will power* you have the power to *make* a decision and
then to *follow it up in practice*. This includes several steps:

- First, you *decide* to do something — such as, to make
  yourself less disturbed and less disturbable:
  "Becoming less upsettable is a valuable quality. I'll try
  my best to achieve it!"
- Second, you are *determined* to act on your decision:
  to do what seems to be required to carry it out: "No
  matter what it takes or how hard it is, I'm going to
  work to make myself less disturbable! I'm quite
  resolved to spare no effort to do this!"
- Third, you *acquire knowledge of* what to do — and
  what not to do — to carry out your will, your decision: "To make myself less disturbed, I will change
  some of my thinking, my feelings, and my behaving.
  Particularly, I will stop whining about the Adversities
  I encounter and stop demanding that they absolutely
  should not and *must not* exist."
- Fourth, you actually start *acting* on your determination and your knowledge: "Instead of telling myself
  that frustrating conditions absolutely must not occur
  in my life, I'll convince myself that these conditions
  must exist when they do exist, that I can cope with
  them, that I can try to change them, and that I can
  accept it, though not like it, when I cannot for the
  present change them. I *can* do this; I *will* do this; now
  let me actually *force myself* to do this. Every time I
  feel horrified about Adversities, I will see that I am
  demanding that they must not exist, and I'll work at
  accepting rather than whining about their existence.
  I'll *change* what I can change and *accept* what I cannot change. I can do this soon. Now let me start
  actually doing it."
- Fifth, you then keep steadily and persistently deciding
  to change, determining to change, acquiring

knowledge about how you can change, and using this knowledge by acting on it. Yes, *acting* to bring change about: "Now that I am working at giving up my demandingness and changing it to a preference, now that I am accepting and no longer whining about bad conditions that I cannot at the present change, I will keep striving along these lines in order to maintain my progress and to keep looking for better ways to help myself, to keep changing, and to keep persisting in my *efforts* and *actions* to change."

- Sixth, if you fall back or relapse to your old non-doing ways — as you may easily do — you decide, once again, to push yourself into more productive paths. You review how to change your ways, you make yourself determined to act on your decision and on your knowledge of how to fulfill it, and then you force yourself to actually execute your decision and your determination, no matter how difficult you may find this action to be and no matter how far and how often you may relapse.

- Seventh, when you do relapse, accept yourself fully with your returned powerlessness and *don't* conclude, "There I go again! What's the use of trying to regain my power?" So restart your self-empowering so that you relapse less and work to overcome your relapsing more quickly in the future. You don't *have to* overcome your relapsing. But that would be nice!

Will power, then, is not merely will, choice, and decision-making — as millions of people wrongly see it as being. Its power includes *determination* to do something, *knowledge* of how to do it, *action* to make yourself do it, *persisting with that action even* when you find it difficult to carry out, and going through this process again — and again! — when you fall back to functioning poorly.

Knowing all this, can you achieve this kind of will power? Indeed, you can — if you have the will power to work at achieving it! You can push yourself, force yourself, impel yourself to choose a goal, be determined to carry it through, gain the knowledge of how to do so, take suitable action to back up your determination and knowledge, force yourself to persist at that action no matter how hard it is, and go through this process again if you fall back to having "weak will power."

As usual, gaining and maintaining will power requires *thought, feeling,* and *behavior.* You had better thoughtfully go over the advantages of gaining it. You can realistically show yourself that it may be hard to achieve it, but it is harder, especially in the long run, if you don't. You can convince yourself that gaining will power requires more than a wish — requires the action to back up this wish. You can do cost-benefit analysis and keep showing yourself that your efforts to achieve will power — such as the steady work you do to acquire it — *are worth the benefits.* On a secondary level, you can convince yourself that failing to gain it is undesirable but not *awful* and that your failure never, of course, makes you an incompetent person or a no-goodnik.

Emotionally, to gain will power you'd better encourage and push yourself by focusing on its gains: on the feeling of strength it gives you, on the power to run your life better, on the pleasures to be gained from it.

Behaviorally, you can fully see that the *power* in will power is in the work, in the effort, in the discomforts that you take on to gain it, and not merely in your thoughts and your feelings. Will power, again, means the action, the work that you do to add power to your will. There may be another way to get it — without work. But I doubt it. Life rarely offers shortcuts!

Loss Is Awful — Or Is It?

Let us assume that you now see what will power is and you are determined to achieve it and apply it to making yourself less disturbable. What now?

First, a few general attitudes you can use to get started on making yourself less disturbable. Later, some more details on achieving these philosophies.

Imagine one of the worst things that can ever happen to you — such as losing all your loved ones, dying of AIDS, or being otherwise truly handicapped and limited. Show yourself that you can still, under these exceptionally bad conditions find some ways in which you can still enjoy yourself. Be really determined to accept, though of course not to like, these grim conditions and to find pleasures, satisfactions, and enjoyments that you can focus upon in spite of your pains and limitations. Don't give up. Assure yourself that in this dreadful situation, which probably will never occur, you can still be reasonably happy at

Puml

times, though not as happy as you would be under less offensive conditions.

Work at convincing yourself — and I mean really convincing yourself — that whatever happens to you and your loved ones, nothing — yes, nothing — is truly *awful* or *terrible*. As noted previously in this book, many things that may occur are bad, painful, frustrating, and against your interest and against the social interest. But nothing will ever be 100 percent bad because it could always be somewhat worse. Nothing will certainly be more than bad. And anything that ever happens that you consider bad will be and *should* be — that is, *has* to be — just as bad as it right now is.

Marilyn was a professor of history and considered herself a realist and a pragmatist. She quickly took very well to REBT when she came to work on her problem of being divorced at the age of 37, having had two miscarriages in the past, and now having no suitable candidate for being the father of the child she very much wanted to bear. She agreed that she didn't absolutely *have to* be a mother but still felt that she would be so greatly deprived if she never bore a child that her tremendous loss would be *awful*. So she was seriously depressed.

Marilyn acknowledged that being childless wouldn't be 100% bad — for she could see that a few things, such as being tortured to death, would be worse. She also agreed that the word *awful* implied *more than bad* — and she could see that remaining childless can't be in that category. But she still insisted that in her case, when she had *such* a great desire for bearing a child, not achieving this goal would truly be *awful*.

At first, I couldn't budge Marilyn and, as time went by with no likelihood of her finding a suitable mate, she became even more depressed. I almost made myself depressed about this!

I persisted with REBT and was able to show Marilyn that calling her loss *bad* made her feel quite sad and sorry, while calling it *awful* made her feel more than sad — depressed. The difference, I pointed out, was that *awful* meant that because her loss was very, very sad, such sadness *should not* exist. And, of course, it did!

Marilyn came up with a rational solution herself: "You're right. *All* degrees of loss and of sadness about my loss *should* definitely exist. I *must* suffer this great deprivation as long as I do. Most unfortunate! But if I call my misfortune *awful* I bring in depression. And that won't help me bear a child or get anything else I want. Now I really see it — and I feel much better already as I say to myself, '*Nothing* is awful unless I define something bad *as* awful. That *definition* does me in!' If I keep telling myself, 'It's very bad, but only bad — and not awful!' I can feel my depression lifting and my sadness remaining. And even great sadness is not *awful!*" With this rational conclusion, Marilyn lost her feeling of depression and persisted at finding a suitable mate.

On Becoming Rational

Don't hang yourself up on distractions, cognitive, emotional, and/or physical. All distractions work to temporarily make you *feel* better. But none of them that I have ever heard of will make you *get* better. No, not meditation, yoga, progressive relaxation, biofeedback, art, music, science, entertainment, nor anything. They all can be useful at diverting you, helping you to focus away from frustration, pain, depression, panic, and horror. But they tend to help you look away from, instead of confronting and eliminating, your own invention and creation of "terror" and "awfulness."

Recognize that there are almost always alternate solutions to your problems and that you can find other enjoyments when some of your main ones are thwarted. Normally, you can find some kinds of satisfactions even when your life is restricted and you can do some kind of problem solving even when you have more than your share of difficulties. So whenever you are in trouble, keep looking for alternate solutions to your problems and possible pleasures that you can still arrange. Don't easily conclude that none exists. This is most, most unlikely!

Take many things seriously — such as work and relationships — *but none of them too seriously.* No good thing *absolutely has* to exist in your life and no bad thing *absolutely must* disappear. Do the best that you can do to cope with frustrations and to improve your lot. But you cannot stem the tides and you cannot perform miracles. It's too darned bad that you are deprived and that you often get what you don't want. Tough! But it's never the end of the world — though you may exaggeratedly think it is. Even then, the world somehow staggers on!

Watch your absolutizing, dogmatizing, overgeneralizing, demanding, and musturbating. Practically all of your preferences, wishes, desires, goals, and values are healthy as long as you do not sacredize them. You can also get along reasonably well in spite of dislikes, distastes, and avoidances — as long as you do not devil-ify them. Making a number of things vitally important and committing yourself to them will add to your existence. But making them crucial, sacred, and a necessity will almost always lead to anxiety, depression, rage, and self-hatred. Be, if you will, devoted — but not dogmatically devout.

Don't expect too much of other people — for they almost always have their own serious problems and are preoccupied mainly with them. Even when they say they cherish you, they are rarely that much on your side. Love them, help them, relate to them, try to win their approval — but never take them *too* seriously. If you accept this, you can greatly enjoy people — or some of them. If you see them as being wholly beneficial or wholly vicious, you'll have trouble!

Unconditionally and fully accept yourself and others. Not what you and they *do*. You will often act foolishly, stupidly, badly, and immorally; and so will they. But do not rate you nor them as *persons*. Do not measure your or their essential *worth*. Accept the sinner but not the sin. Hate your and other people's "bad" thoughts, acts, and feelings but not the person, the human, who performs these "bad" acts. I shall return to unconditional self-acceptance (USA) in more detail in the next chapter.

Recognize that you were born and raised with very strong tendencies to be self-actualizing as well as self-defeating. You are able to think straight, to be realistic and logical, and to figure out better solutions for yourself and others. But you are also prone to go for short-range instead of long-range gains, to damn yourself and other people, to insist that everyone must treat you fairly and considerately, and often to sabotage yourself and others.

Once you habituate yourself to destructive behavior, you may have great difficulty in changing. Once you create or accept harmful ideas, you may rigidly hold on to them and have trouble in giving them up. So avoiding foolish behavior is often difficult, and indulging in it quite easy! However, as noted above, you can change yourself — with hard work and practice. So forcefully, vigorously, powerfully determine to use your constructive tendencies to minimize your destructive ones; and then forcefully, vigorously, powerfully, and persistently work at creating better thinking, healthier feelings, and more productive actions. Do this now, not later; and keep working at it for the rest of your charming life!

You're Incurable!

While steadily working for your own and for others' health and happiness, give up the concept of cure. You never get cured, nor cure yourself, of the human condition. You always, always, always will be fallible, error-prone, and subject to self-defeating thoughts and actions. You never recover from human nature. You can, if you follow the ideas in this book, make yourself and keep yourself much less disturbed and more self-actualizing. You may bring yourself to the point where you rarely seriously upset yourself about anything — yes, anything. But not completely. Not absolutely. Not a hundred percent. If you believe in total cure, moreover, you will stop working when you reach a certain point, and will tend to let yourself fall back. So forget utopia. Forget perfectionism. Try for *your* best rather than *the* best. You'll never be totally rational, sane, nor sensible. Does that include me, too? In a word, yes!

Sometimes try self-help methods and psychotherapy first. But don't reject possible medication. Experiment. See what works for you. Watch out for the gurus and the other fanatics who swear by esoteric and miracle cures. Seek counsel with trained professionals and not with New Age crackpots. When anyone offers you a quick, easy, miracle cure and has no scientific data to back it up, run, run, run to the nearest and best professional you can find. Check it out!

6

Accepting Yourself and Others

We now come to the heart of this book. If you have read it carefully so far, you have seen that you are born and reared to be easily disturbable. Yes, to make yourself think, feel, and act self-defeatingly. Handily. Often. No trouble at all!

You are also born and reared with strong constructive, problem-solving tendencies. Luckily! So you can use these, as we have noted, to observe what you do to upset yourself, to find your fiendishly clever self-sabotaging ways, and to devise effective methods of changing. Yes, you *can* largely pull yourself up with your own thinking, feeling, and action bootstraps. If you *choose* to do so. If you *work* at doing so.

So use some of the methods I have described so far. Try other techniques too. Rational Emotive Behavior Therapy (REBT) is comprehensive but not exactly exhaustive. You can find, through your own experience and study, other methods besides the many included in this book. Look for them. Try them out. Discover what works for you.

As I show in more detail later, most therapy methods are usable but limited. They help fine — for awhile. They soften your upsetness — but leave some of its deeper roots. They help you *feel* better but not *get* better.

On, now, to some deeper methods. How can you make yourself *much* less disturbed? How can you reduce your *general* anxiety, depression, and rage? If you are now mainly upset about, say, work or money, how can you decrease your other disturbances — about relationships, addictions, or whatever? How can you make yourself less distur*bable* about practically *any* unfortunate events that may occur in your future life? How indeed!

The previous chapter, I hope, gave you some inkling about making yourself less disturbable. The present chapter urges you much further along this road — fills in important details that I glossed over a little too quickly and lightly.

I shall now describe some of the most effective methods of achieving mental health that I have discovered in my personal life, as well as by working for over a half century with tens of thousands of my therapy clients and my workshop participants. Every one of the following techniques has significantly helped many people to achieve remarkable changes in their lives. None of them, however, has helped everyone. Which ones are for you? Try them and see!

Strong But Realistic Expectations of Changing Yourself

As Jerome Frank, Simon Budman, Russell Grieger, Otto Rank, Paul Woods, and other well-known therapists have noted, therapy works when clients definitely expect that they can and will change. Right. But your expectations had better not be unrealistic and Pollyannaish. If you have over-optimistic, magical attitudes about any therapy — and about your "great" therapist — you will expect too much, be disappointed and disillusioned, and may give up trying to it.

So, too, with self-help methods. Be optimistic, but not unrealistic about them. They will provide you with no miracle cure, no easy way out of your neurotic difficulties. But have confidence that they *may* work.

This goes for REBT and CBT. Be skeptical about them. Investigate their track record. Not just through anecdotal case histories, which are often largely fiction. Most of Freud's early cases, for example, were beautifully written and sound quite convincing. But later investigation showed that some of his famous patients (such as Anna O) were wrongly diagnosed, rarely improved, and even got worse.

In the case of REBT and CBT, the record so far is unusually good. If we skip the anecdotal histories of their "successes" — like those frequently reported by psychoanalysts — and if we stick to the hundreds of studies where they have been used with a control group that had no therapy or a different form of therapy, we find that they are among the most confirmed therapies of all time. Behavior therapy itself has an excellent record in this regard; but it has been used with a limited range of problems.

REBT and CBT have been used with people with some of the worst forms of anxiety, depression, and rage and have been quite effective. No perfect results, of course, and no miracles. But unusually good tested results — and hundreds of them. If you want to check out some of the efficacy research studies of REBT you can look at the references by H. Barlow, A.T. Beck, D. Hajzler and M. Bernard; L. Lyons and and P. Woods; T.E. McGovern and M.S. Silverman; and M.S. Silverman, M. McCarthy and T.E. Mc Govern, found in the back of this book.

You can therefore use REBT with a good degree of confidence that it often works, and may well be able to work for you. Convince yourself that you can understand it, apply it, and have a good chance to make yourself distinctly less disturbable. Why so? For three important reasons:

- According to REBT, you have little control over many unfortunate Activating Events or Adversities (A's) that plague you, but you largely can control your Beliefs (B's) about these Adversities. Fortunately, you largely become disturbed not because of your *preferences* for success and approval but because of your raising these into absolutistic *musts.*

  You *can* control and change your own disturbance-creating demands! Even when you have strongly believed and acted upon them for many years, REBT shows you that you are disturbed today largely because you still (consciously and unconsciously) *choose* to hold them, and that you definitely have the ability and power to change them, and sometimes entirely give them up.

- REBT gives you quite a number of thought-, emotion-, and action-oriented methods of understanding and changing your dogmatic musts and the harmful behaviors that often accompany them. You can actively and forcefully Dispute them — realistically, logically, and pragmatically — and greatly reduce them.

- If you keep giving up your grandiose demands on yourself, on others, and on the world, you can minimize your *tendency* to think and feel them. You can change your disturbed views that you are worthless, that people who treat you unfairly should be shot at dawn, and that the whole world is rotten. Once you *see* your commands as harmful, *see* that you can change them, and actually do modify them, you can retain your new attitudes fairly automatically.

If you have realistic expectations of what you can do to help yourself with REBT, you can come up with attitudes like these:

"I am naturally an upsettable person, who sometimes needlessly disturbs myself. I do so mainly by taking my goals and preferences and escalating them to grandiose demands. It is foolish and self-defeating when I do this, but I can unconditionally accept myself with this behavior, and not call myself a fool for indulging in it. Because I largely make myself disturbed, I also can see this and undisturb myself. I can vigorously Dispute my demandingness and by forcefully acting to uproot it, I now clearly see several ways out of my neuroticism. I can therefore eagerly, confidently look forward to using REBT for the rest of my life. If I continue to do this, I will make myself less disturbable, will rarely upset myself needlessly, and if I fall back I can look for my godlike commands again and forcefully change them back to sensible preferences. I can!"

If you acquire this self-helping philosophy, if you have realistic expectations of how you can refuse to disturb yourself, and if you keep determined to use a number of REBT methods to do so, you won't guarantee your becoming less disturbable. But you will probably be well on your way!

Unconditional Self-Acceptance (USA)

You really only have two choices of self-acceptance — to accept yourself conditionally or unconditionally. The first choice won't work.

Conditional self-acceptance is one of the greatest sicknesses known to man and woman. Not to mention children and adolescents! It means that you only accept yourself *under certain conditions* — when, for example, you succeed at important projects, win the approval of significant people, or contribute nicely to society. Sounds good, doesn't it? But it's really deadly. For several reasons:

When you *don't* fulfill the conditions you have decided that you *absolutely must* fulfill for "self-worth," you're obviously worthless, no good, a cretin, a lump of manure. However! — as a fallible human, you frequently *won't* succeed at important projects. You will *fail* to win the approval of significant people. You will *not* contribute nicely to society. Take my word for it — unless you are truly perfect and completely lucky — you often

won't. Not by a long shot. When you fail, and you do not _____
the conditions you set for your "self-esteem," you will "logically"
conclude that you are a worm, and almost always feel anxious
and depressed. Why? Because you define your self, your "worth"
in terms of these *conditions*. When you do what you do mainly
for the enjoyment of doing it, you create much less anxiety —
and paradoxically are likely to do it better!

While you are trying to fulfill the conditions you set for self-
approval — "I am only O.K. *when* I succeed, *when* I win
approval, *when* I help others" — you can't help worrying about
not meeting these "necessary" conditions: "Suppose I *fail* at this
important project...?" "What if I *don't* win John's (or Joan's)
love...?" "Suppose I try hard to help others and I'm *unable* to do
so or suppose I even *harm* them...!" With thoughts like these,
which are almost inevitable, you'll worry, worry, worry and help
yourself *un*achieve the goals that you think you *must* attain to
make yourself a "worthwhile" person. And because you have not
yet met your "necessary" goals, you often will think you *deserve*
worthlessness. Catch 22!

Even when you marvelously succeed at fulfilling the
conditions that will presumably make you a "good" individual,
how can you assure yourself that you will *continue* to succeed?
You can't. Obviously, you can always fail *later*. "Now that I'm
succeeding at this important project, will I keep doing so
tomorrow?" "Yes, John (or Joan) loves me today, but will he (or
she) *still* love me a year from now?" So, once again, you will
worry, worry, worry!

Rating yourself as a *good person* because you do *good acts* is
purely *definitional*. Anyone could come along and easily disagree
with you — could say, for example, that you still are "bad"
because (1) You are not perfect; (2) you do not perform *well
enough*; (3) you just are, as a human, *no damned good*; or (4)
your "good" acts are *really* "bad." Then where are you? In doubt.
For who is *really* right — you or this other definer of your
goodness? Who can say? No one!

Self-esteem, then — or any *conditional* measurement of your
self, your *being*, your *essence*, or your *personhood* — simply
won't work. Nor, as Alfred Korzybski showed in 1933 in *Science
and Sanity*, can *self*-rating be accurate. There *is*, he said, no *is*
of identity: "Identity is invariably false to facts." For if you *are* a
"good" person, you would have to be totally, globally "good" at *all*
times and under *all* conditions. Who, you included, can actually

be 100% good — or, for that matter, bad? No one! Even a "good act" — such as helping someone in pain — cannot always, only, and under all conditions *be* good. Sometimes it may lead to harmful results. For example, you may help a murderer, who may later slay a dozen people! You may help an accident victim in the wrong way, so that he or she is harmed.

If you want to be wise — or, more accurately, act wisely much of the time — you will refrain from rating your *self*, your *being*, your *personhood* at all. Yes, at all! You will establish important goals and purposes — such as remaining alive and being happy when alone, with others, at work, and at play. When you fail to fulfill these goals or purposes — for example, fail in a relationship — you can say, "*This* is bad." And when you succeed, you can say, "*This* is good." But you can and had better refrain from inaccurately — and self-defeatingly — saying, "*I* am good" or "*I* am bad." Making a mistake doesn't make *you* a mistake!

This is one of the most important lessons that REBT teaches. You, your personhood, are never measurable, or capable of being globally evaluated. Once you establish purposes or goals in your life — which you had better choose to survive and be happy! — you can realistically believe that your *thoughts*, *feelings*, or *acts* are good when they promote your chosen goals. And you can sensibly believe that any of your *behaviors* are bad when they block or sabotage your goals. But you never — no, never — need choose to foolishly Believe, "*I* am good" or "*I* am bad."

Instead, you can choose to assert, "I am a *person*, a *unique individual*, who is now alive and capable of enjoying myself. Now how do I find pleasures that will not later harm me and my social group and how do I avoid pains and continue to have a happy life *without* giving a global rating to my *self* or my *personhood*?"

Good! But let me warn you: It is difficult for you to have a "self" or "identity," to rate what you *do* to fulfill your purposes, and *not* to evaluate this "self." As a human, you were born and raised to rate your efforts and your deeds — first, to help you survive and, second, to get along with the members of your social group. So that is fine.

But, but, but! You were also taught to rate, and have a biological tendency to evaluate your *self*, your *you-ness*. So just try to reduce this propensity! You can — but only with much effort and practice. You are a *natural* self-rater. Even when you *only* appraise your behaviors for awhile, you may easily slip back to harmful *self*-evaluation.

REBT, therefore, offers you an easy solution to your problem of self-rating. How? By defining yourself as "a good person" just because you are alive and human. Yes, for *no* other reason. Doing this, you say to yourself — very *strongly* say to yourself — "I am good, I am worthy, I am okay *just* because I exist, *just* because I am human, *just* because I *choose* to view myself as good." Period.

Convince yourself of this *powerfully*. With *feeling*. If you fully believe this, you will achieve *un*conditional self-acceptance (USA). For your conditions are *always* fulfilled. Obviously, you now exist. Obviously, you are human. Obviously, you can *choose* to view yourself as good just because you are alive and are human. If so, you can constantly fulfill the conditions that you set up as requirements for your "goodness." Clever! Until you are dead, non-human, or stop defining yourself as "good," you can't lose.

So this practical or pragmatic solution to the problem of self-worth is okay. If you use it, it will work. You'll never view yourself as a bad person, a no-goodnik. Unless you "choose" to do so after you are dead!

However, this solution, "I am always okay just because I am alive and human," has a real weakness — because it is not a fact but a *definition*. Using it, you can easily *say* that you are always "good" and never "bad," but anybody else can say otherwise. Neither you nor your objectors can scientifically *prove* you are right. Nor can you or they *falsify* your position. So where are you? Philosophically, on somewhat flimsy ground.

So REBT gives you another choice. You can set up goals and purposes (such as living and enjoying) and only rate your thoughts, feelings, and actions as "good" when they help you achieve these goals — and as "bad" when they block your chosen goals. You can refuse to globally measure or evaluate your *self*, your *essence*, or your *being* at all. Yes, not at all! Merely concentrate on enjoying your life and *not* on proving how good or how bad you *are*.

Why is your giving yourself unconditional self-acceptance (USA) so important? Because when you lack it you often addict yourself to self-downing. You damn yourself for your mistakes, failures, stupidities, and defects. All of which, as a fallible person, you frequently have.

Worse! — you damn yourself for the results of damning yourself: for the feelings of anxiety and depression that self-reproach produces. You hate your mood swings — but you also hate *you* for having mood swings.

You also, frequently, become defensive about your faults. Thus, you damn yourself for failing at love or work and you then feel so upset that you *can't stand* your self-hatred. So you deny and rationalize, claim that you really *didn't* fail, refuse to learn from your failures, and you help yourself fail some more.

Or you blame your partner or boss or lover for *making* you fail. You then create feelings of rage (damning others) for their evil ways. Now you are very angry, defensive — and still blaming yourself underneath. Then, if you see how harmful your rage is, you may berate yourself for feeling enraged.

If you work hard at achieving USA and get to the point where you rarely condemn yourself for *anything* you do — while admitting your poor behaviors — you will still have a healthy ego — "I, a unique individual, exist, and *I* will try to do well, have good relationships, help others, and feel happy." But you will reduce your harmful ego-*rating.* And the disturbability that it keeps setting it aflame.

Unconditional Acceptance Of Others (UAO)

You, alas, are a fallible and often screwed-up human. So is everyone else! Other people will often treat you shabbily, obnoxiously, unfairly, and unjustly. Why? Because they will! That's the way things are, as the whole history of the human race demonstrates.

People usually won't see their actions as "bad." Or they will think you "deserve" how badly they treat you. Or they will admit their wrongs and still keep perpetrating them. Or whatever!

So look for one of your common Irrational Beliefs: "Because people *preferably should not* act as rotten as they do, *they absolutely must not* act that way!" For how, indeed, could people *not* act badly right now when they clearly *are* acting badly? Where is it written that they *must* act nicely when, according to you, they unquestionably are not?

No nonsense now! Whenever you are sorely displeased with others' behaviors, that is your personal prerogative. But you are incredibly grandiose when you demand that people *cannot* act as you dislike and that you *can't stand* it if they do. People can, of course, behave any way they choose to behave. And if you really *couldn't stand* it, you would die because of their actions. Well, how often will you die?

So take care! Hate, if you will, what other people often *do* — or what they fail to do. But don't *demand* that they act nicely. Don't damn *them*, their total personality, for their "rotten" *actions*. Try to help them, unangrily, to change. But when they won't (or occasionally, can't) change, accept *them* as fallible humans. Accept the sinner, even when they continue to "sin." Don't forget — but still forgive.

Anger, rage, and fury are difficult to overcome because they often make your ego feel good. You put others down — and you go up on the emotional see-saw. You feel strong and powerful when you are enraged — even though you are weakly covering up your vulnerability or yielding to childish temper tantrums. You feel as if you are a *better person* than your target is — because you, of course, are *completely right* while he or she is wrong, rotten, no good. You *rule* over your enemy — and presumably everyone else *knows* what a great ruler you are. You make up for your previous mistakes and weaknesses by showing how *unquestionably* right and righteous you now are.

Actually, anger and rage show your weakness. They make you dogmatic, out of control, impulse-ridden. They drive you into overgeneralizing, to making foolish decisions, to wasting time and energy, to obsessing yourself with people you hate, to losing friends, to antagonizing people you love, and to doing crazy, destructive and sometimes even criminal acts. They take a great physical toll — often bringing on undue stress, high blood pressure, intestinal problems, cardiac disabilities, and worsening of other physical problems. Anger and rage mainly interfere with efficient problem- solving, short-range and long-range planning, success-seeking, sports accomplishments, and other constructive pursuits.

Giving up your rage and gaining unconditional acceptance of others (UAO) involves a profound philosophical change that may greatly enhance your life. It shows you that you *can* control some of your strongest, natural, and destructive feelings. It gives you real peace — with others *and* with yourself. It enriches friendship, love, collaboration, cooperation, and creativity. It leads to working better, and to more enjoyable, interesting and valuable projects. It presents a fine model to your intimates, associates, and peers. It encourages and often creates peace on earth, good will to men and women. And longer life!

As I noted before, when you put yourself down, you often feel so bad that you consciously or unconsciously weasel out by blaming others. Not so good! When you damn others for their poor behaviors, you also may reinforce your own blaming tendencies and get too strongly on your own back: "I see that *they're* no good for acting stupidly, but because I too, act that way doesn't that also make *me* a worm?" According to the "logic" of self-rating, the answer is: Yes.

Again: when you denounce others you may note their hurt, their return anger, their lack of love and cooperation, and their moves against you. And you may note your own over-reaction and lack of control — and may down yourself for this.

Achieving unconditional acceptance of others (UAO) is profound, is healthy self-control, is far-reaching. Especially when some of these others *do* act abominably. By gaining UAO, you fully acknowledge that you create and manage — and often fail to manage — your feelings. UAO is honest, realistic, practical. It puts you in the driver's seat with yourself — and, often with your peers. If you see this, work at achieving UAO, and actually do achieve it many times, it becomes automatic through practice. You then *easily* think, feel, and act unfuriously. You clearly govern yourself. Not always — but in a big sense, forever. You're at peace with you — and much more fully at peace with the world.

Make yourself see this. Decide to achieve this. Determine to act on your decision. Act, act, and act on it. Make your will into *will power* to increase your UAO. For your *and* the social good.

Greg, a 27-year-old salesman, got considerable joy from lambasting other people and thus feeling good about himself. Unfortunately, his rage at others raised his blood pressure and started to lead to tension-created back pain. At first, he refused to accept the REBT view that when people treated him unfairly, it was his irrational demands that such people must not be the way they were, and not the unfairness itself, that created his anger at them. When I got him to experimentally accept this view, he was amazed to find how swiftly and greatly his rage diminished. His back pain not only ebbed but he was overwhelmed with such an embracing feeling of peacefulness that he could hardly believe that he has reached it. For the first time in his life he felt good about himself *because* he felt good about himself — and not because he was putting others down beneath him.

7

It's Awful! It's Terrible! It's Horrible! I Can't Stand It!

Life is spelled h-a-s-s-l-e for just about everyone. What do we frequently encounter from the cradle to the grave? Hundreds — sometimes thousands — of pains, diseases, afflictions, ailments, frustrations, restrictions, disappointments, problems, handicaps, injustices, fights, financial difficulties, rejections, criticisms, put-downs, barriers, prejudices, etc.

Why is it that, very often, our fondest wishes are blocked and our worst abhorrences fulfilled? Because they simply are. Need this perpetually happen? Yes, indeed. None of us, even when we are well cared for as children, escape trials and tribulations. And as adolescents and adults? Forget it!

What can you do to stop enraging and depressing yourself about life's "horrors?" Obviously — de-horrify them. To add to what Reinhold Niebuhr wisely said in the beginning of the twentieth century, give yourself the courage to change the unfortunate things you can change, the serenity to accept (but not to like) what you can't change, and the wisdom to know the difference. Thus can you stubbornly refuse to make horrors and terrors out of rotten inconveniences.

But *real* difficulty, *great* trouble often exists. You and your relatives may personally suffer from serious diseases, injuries, assault and violence, crime, and other problems; and if you look at TV and your newspaper every day, you will find gruesome details of floods, famine, terrorism, wars, genocide, and other atrocities. Obviously, however, not everyone who suffers, suffers about this kind of suffering. Not everyone *defines* bad things as *awful*, *terrible*, and *horrible* — and thereby usually makes them worse. Many do, most often do. But not everyone does. And no one does all the time.

Why do you awfulize about inconveniences — and thereby increase your woes? Perhaps because you inherit this tendency from early ancestors who couldn't live *too* peacefully and lazily, or else they'd die. To survive, they may have developed a dramatic "horror" about dangers and thus impelled themselves into preventive action.

Perhaps, along with these kinds of security operations, early humans discovered that verbal awfulizing — whining and complaining about how *terrible* bad things were — enlisted support from others, which may have led to survival of the most self-pitying.

No matter. Awfulizing exists on a world wide scale and may well be an inherent reaction to very bad, potentially fatal events. Who among us doesn't fairly often engage in it? Few!

Awfulizing, moreover, has some benefits. When you view an Adversity (A) as *awful* and *horrible*, you attend to it closely, give thought to changing or escaping from it, and often take preventive actions that you might not otherwise take. Sometimes it spurs you to save your and your loved ones' lives. It thereby may — I say *may* — aid human survival.

But not a very happy survival! What we call nature doesn't care too much *how* we survive — as long as we do. It therefore encourages us thin-skinned vulnerable animals to be *highly* cautious, vigilant, and anxious when faced with danger, and to run like hell from perceived hazards. In fact, because of our nature we often see *greater* dangers than may actually exist. So we survive — often miserably with too much panic and flight. But we *do* survive!

So awfulizing often works. But non-awfulizing about very bad things usually works better. As REBT holds, you have a *choice* of negative feelings when you're faced with dangers. You can make yourself, first, feel *healthily* concerned and vigilant; and second, *unhealthily* panicked and horrified. The first choice will almost always help you more than the second choice. For several reasons:

Panic and horror, which accompany awfulizing, are disruptive and interfere with your finding good solutions to serious problems. They sometimes stun you, so you can't think straight. They may help you run away from "horror" faster — but in the wrong direction. They propel you to make quick solutions which are often quite poor. They knock out of your mind better, alternative solutions. They sometimes disrupt your physical responses and zap your energy. They make you *feel* weak and out of control, and encourage self-downing about your weakness.

How can you *not* see things as *awful* when, as almost anyone will agree with you, they are indeed very bad? Not easily! Very bad things may indeed afflict you and your loved ones. For example: Loss of sight, limbs, hearing, or your kidneys or intestines. Child abuse, incest, rape, assault, serious victimization. Poverty, crime, discrimination, sexual and other harassment. Severe mental and emotional disturbances. Et cetera!

Nonetheless, exceptionally bad occurrences are only *awful*, *horrible* or *terrible* when you define them as such. *Bad* never really means *awful* but you may *think* it does. And you never *have to* think in that self-destructive way. In fact, if you think clearly, you'll soon see that nothing — no, nothing — is *awful*. Because *awful* normally has several meanings, most of them inaccurate. Two of its accurate meanings are:

1. *Awful* means quite bad or extremely bad. Well, that's almost always, by your own standards and goals, correct. If you strongly prefer to succeed at sex, love, work, or sports and you actually fail and get rejected, your failure is obviously against your interest — and therefore it is *frustrating* or *bad*. Not necessarily to others, of course; but certainly to you. So to evaluate your failing or being rejected as *bad* seems accurate enough.

2. You can legitimately call something very bad if it is greatly against your goals and interests. Thus, if you fail so badly at an important project that it seems certain that you'll *never* succeed at it, you can say that this failure is *very* bad or *highly* frustrating. For example, if you fail to win the love of the one person you truly care for and it looks like you'll never win a partner who is equally good, you can say that this is a *very* bad loss.

So these two Adversities, if you call them *awful*, almost fit that term. When, however, you say that some other kind of Adversity is *awful* or *horrible*, you usually mean several other things that you cannot realistically prove. Look, for example, at these illegitimate and self-defeating definitions of *awful*:

1. By calling a *bad* event *awful* you really mean that it's *so* bad that it absolutely *should not, must not* ever exist. But this is ridiculous — because no matter *how* bad it is it *does* exist and it *has to* exist when it does. So you are grandiosely demanding that only moderately bad things should occur but that very bad things have absolutely no right to happen. In fact, when you call

them *awful*, you are contradictorily claiming that they clearly *do* exist but that they indubitably *must* not. How odd!

2. When you insist that an undesirable event is *awful* or *terrible*, you are implying — if you're honest with yourself — that it is *as bad as it could be*: completely or 100% bad. But actually nothing can be 100% bad, because it invariably could be *worse*. If you are raped and killed, that is very bad, but not 100% bad, because several of your loved ones could *also* be raped and slaughtered, and that would be worse. If you are tortured to death slowly, you could always be tortured to death *slower*. About the only thing that could really be *totally* bad would be the annihilation of the entire human race, all the living and non-living things that now exist, and the whole universe. Well, that hardly seems likely in the near future.

Even if our entire universe were to be annihilated, that would be most unfortunate but not really *awful*, for several reasons: (a) We all ultimately will die anyway, (b) Once we were destroyed, we wouldn't *know* that we were non-existent, (c) It is sad that many species — like tyrannosaurus Rex and the dinosaur — no longer exist, but is it really *awful?* (d) If you view possible or actual human (or animal) annihilation, as *awful*, how will that help you stay alive or be happy?

3. When you label a very unfortunate occurrence as *horrible*, *terrible*, or *awful*, you sometimes imply — if, again, you are really honest — that it is *more than bad,* — 101% or perhaps 200% bad. How are you going to prove *that* supposition?

4. When you claim that a very bad happening is *awful*, you often mean that it is *so* impossibly bad that it (a) illegitimately exists, (b) must not be *as* bad as it indubitably is, (c) absolutely must not exist *at all*, and (d) is so *frightfully* bad that you cannot effectively change it, or accept it, or cope with it. In the course of having these highly contradictory thoughts about badness you tend to simultaneously deify and devil-ify it; insist that it is *too* real as well as *un*real; and thereby interfere with your dealing with it. What a tangled mess your awfulizing creates!

5. As noted above, awfulizing will very rarely help you (or anyone!) make bad things better, and will frequently interfere with your improving them. You will *feel* that things are *more* frustrating and *worse* than they actually are; and you may actually aggravate them. By dwelling on them you will also *increase* and *perpetuate* their annoyingness. You will endlessly plague yourself with them.

The solution to awfulizing? Convince yourself that badness is *only* bad, not awful. Even *very* bad is still just bad, never more than bad. *Accept* obnoxious happenings as you keep trying to change them. Keep uncreating *horrors* and *terrors* until you truly no longer believe in them. Then you will tend to automatically stop from creating them and, when you occasionally do fabricate them again, you will quickly change them back to mere badness. After doing this enough times, you will still feel frustrated and disappointed about real Adversities — and frustrated enough to try to improve them. But you will practically never make hassles into catastrophes, nor real misfortunes into fictional horrors.

Reduce I-Can't-Stand-It-Itis

Like practically all humans, when you greatly don't like something that is happening to you, you often tend to foolishly insist, "I *can't stand* it! I *can't bear* it!" But you really *can* and *do*. Why? Because, first, if you really *couldn't stand* painful events — such as failing to find a good job, being rejected by someone for whom you care, or suffering from a serious illness — you would presumably die of such losses. Well, *will* you? Not unless you stupidly kill yourself. Maybe you truly can't stand falling off a high cliff and still survive. But very few things you don't like will actually kill you. In fact, you rarely say, "I *can't stand it!*" when you are referring to physical danger — but mainly to non-dangerous events like rejection. So you *can* stand practically everything that you don't at all like.

Second, Beliefs — such as "I *can't stand* losing this fine job!" or "I *can't bear* losing John's (or Joan's) love!" — are vast exaggerations. They really mean, "If or when I lose this fine job or lose John's (or Joan's) love, as I *absolutely must not*, I can't thereafter be happy *at all* and I must experience *only* enormous pain and misery practically every minute for the rest of my life!" Well?! You can probably *make* this Belief true by profoundly *believing* and *acting* on it. But is it *really* true? Do you *have* to make yourself anguished *forever* when something seriously goes wrong in your life? You *can*, of course, but you clearly don't *have* to. You *can* find other enjoyments. If you *decide* to do so.

Third, whenever you say, "I *can't stand* this!" or "I *can't bear* that!" you are, in fact, still living and actually standing it. If you say, "I can't stand this job!" or "I can't tolerate this marriage!" you can plot and plan to leave it. Fine. That's sensible *determination* to change the situation. But when you *can't stand it* and miserably *stay* in a job or a marriage, you are actually bearing it and are whining that you can't bear what in fact you *are* bearing!

Yes, bad happenings, and even very bad happenings, will keep occurring. But you can *choose* to deal with them and choose to find some other satisfactions. Or you can choose to "not stand" them, still stay, and make yourself needlessly suffer! Also, you can choose to leave a situation which would have been better for you *had* you stood it and *had* you done something to improve it.

Why is it of crucial — though not of *absolute* — importance that you solidly, strongly, steadily believe, "I definitely *can* stand just about *anything*, no matter how much I dislike it!"? For several reasons:

1. You will often experience unfavorable happenings. To preserve yourself, you had better realistically define them as Adversities, and do your best to reduce or eliminate them. Poverty, for example. Being assaulted and raped. Serious disease and accidents. Imprisonment and torture. You had better *healthily* detest these events, plan to ward them off, enlist the aid of others, stop contributing to them yourself and deal with them when you can't avoid them. But *not* resort to *I-can't-stand-it-itis*, which often raises your feelings of loathing and hinders your coping abilities.

2. "I can't bear this Adversity!" implies that you can hardly tolerate contemplating it and planning to diminish it. If so, how can you then deal with it and/or change it?

3. I-can't-stand-it-itis tends to make you think crookedly and act disruptively about people and events that you find obnoxious. If you think you *can't stand* critical people, you will most likely make yourself feel angry at them, exaggerate their "wrongs," block yourself from being assertive, and overdo your complaints against them. Where will any of these behaviors get you? Not likely to act constructively!

4. When you *can't stand* someone's actions, you make yourself *overly* upset about them — and often see them as worse than they are. When you *can't stand* people who act obnoxiously, you often damn them for their poor behavior, conclude that they are totally no good, and perhaps boycott them completely and lose out on their good traits. You make yourself so bigoted that you will often find evil in some of their good and neutral actions.

5. Similarly, when you *can't stand* a bad situation — such as a family or work event — you are likely to see it as *all* bad and

no good, to boycott it completely, and to lose out on its good and enjoyable aspects.

When you fully convince yourself that you *can* stand frustrating people and events, you can choose to leave them or to stay with them and can enjoy their good features. Moreover, you sometimes had better not avoid Adversities — as when you have in-laws you can't easily boycott, a rotten boss but a fine and well-paying job, or a disease like cancer. You can still *accept* their unpleasantness, in some cases find aspects of them that you can appreciate, and put up with them and find other satisfying commitments.

Once you, again, fully convince yourself that you can stand almost *anything* that occurs and you will erase the *horror* of living and be stuck only with its great and small *inconveniences*. When you strongly believe that you can *only* experience various discomforts and that nothing is *more than* inconvenient, you may achieve unusual serenity. Yes: Still determined to change harmful things you can change, but serenely abiding — sometimes enjoying — what you cannot. This unusual kind of level-headedness can lastingly color your life. Elegantly!

Avoid Overgeneralizing and Labeling

People easily generalize — and almost as easily overgeneralize. Because you failed to get several jobs you were after, you may rightly conclude, "Most of the jobs I want are not available to me. I guess I'd better try for a good many, so that I finally get one that I prefer."

Good! That's a sensible generalization. It will help you.

But you can foolishly add, "Because I keep failing to get a job I want, I'll *never* get a good one. *No* desirable positions are available to me. I'd better give up and stop trying to get one."

Because you failed several times, you *don't* have to fail this time. Because your bright blue-eyed father or mother did you in, don't think you must avoid *all* bright blue-eyed people. You may find it difficult to understand and talk with *most* devout religionists. But with *all* of them?

Your overgeneralizations are illogical and self-limiting. And they may create prejudices against other individuals and groups. Check and revise them.

An especially harmful form of overgeneralizing consists of *labeling*. If you say, "I *am* lazy" or "I *am* a lazy person," you take *some* of your behavior and imply that you *always* and in practically *all* areas, act lazily. But do you? Labeling also implies that you will fit a particular label forever and that you cannot change. If you really *are* lazy — that is, have a lazy *core* — how can you possibly push yourself to be less lazy or unlazy? Not very well!

"I *am* lazy," moreover, frequently implies, "And I *shouldn't* be that way, and am *no good* for being as lazy as I *should* not be!" Here again, as I previously noted, you are using the *is* of identity and are implying that *you* are always bad when some of your behavior some of the time is less desirable than you would like it to be.

Even telling yourself, "I act lazily," can have hazards. For it may imply that you act lazily about practically everything almost all of the time. Is that true? Hardly!

Also! Be careful about labeling yourself with some *aspects* of your disturbances. You have, perhaps, depressed feelings — at certain times and under specific conditions. But if you therefore conclude "I *am* a depressive," you encourage yourself to *practically always* feel depressed under *many* conditions. This is one of the dangers of our medical tradition — that we often label people as *depressives* and thereby discourage them from even *trying* to change.

Similarly, statements like "I am screwed up" are much worse than, "I behave in a screwed up manner some of the time." "He is a nut!" is vastly different from, "As far as I can see, he acts nuttily in some ways on a number of special kinds of occasions."

Is all labeling foolish? Definitely not. Both a banana and a pear may be called "a fruit," and no great harm will be done. But if you say, "Because bananas and pears are fruit, and because I dislike both of them I'd better stay away from *all* fruit," you then may be in trouble. Restricting and damning overgeneralizations are the ones to watch out for. So carefully assess destructive behavior but not the person, including yourself!, who performs it.

Don't, however, cop out and resign. When people behave "badly" and "unjustly" — as they often will! — give up your godlike commands that they *have* to desist, stop damning *them* for their "rotten" *behaviors*, try to *unangrily* induce them to change, and *accept* (without *liking*) what they still won't change. Nonetheless, tell them, if feasible, why and how you'd *like* them to behave instead. Persuade them — *unfuriously* — to act better. Choose, if you can, to stay away from them. But stop screaming and whining that they must not do what they're unquestionably doing. If you have the power to stop them, carefully use it. If you have no power over them, don't pretend that you do have it. People will often act the way they want, not the way that you want. Too bad — but not *awful!*

To make a profound philosophical change, and thereby to make yourself less disturbable, you had better see what Alfred Korzybski pointed out in *Science and Sanity* in 1933: You, like the rest of us humans, have an innate and acquired powerful tendency to often overgeneralize and to incorporate labeling, the *is* of identity, either/or thinking, and other inaccuracies into your language. This won't make you insane but, as Korzybski noted, it will often help you be unsane — or neurotic.

Kevin Everett FitzMaurice, a therapist in Omaha, Nebraska, has been one of the leading therapists to apply General Semantics principles to psychotherapy and counseling. His *Attitude Is All You Need* contains some excellent points against generalizing and labeling. He agrees with the REBT principles that you had better avoid absolutistic shoulding and musting, damning yourself, whining, blaming others, and demanding that others change. He adds to these rational principles: Stop reifying! Reifying means taking your thought about a bad thing (such as failing) and viewing this thought *as* the thing. Thus, because you *view* failure as "horrible," you make it into a thought-thing and are sure that, in its own right, it *is* "horrible." Actually, it is only "horrible" to you. But your view, and your strong feeling about its "horror" makes it "unquestionably horrible." You then *act* as if failure *is* "horrible," and get yourself into all kinds of needless trouble!

You can use general semantics, Kevin E. FitzMaurice's concept of thought-things, and what REBT calls overgeneralized, crooked thinking to see how you easily give yourself emotional problems; and you may thereby help yourself arrive at "elegant" solutions to your disturbances.

Try to see when you are overgeneralizing, labeling, and using either/or instead of and/also language. Reducing your semantic carelessness is no panacea for mental health but will reduce your absolutism and dogma. The more alert you are to language-encouraged disturbance the less prone you will become to self-defeating thinking, feeling, and behaving. After awhile, you'll often catch yourself *before* you open your big mouth and speak inaccurately to yourself and others. If so, you will then be significantly less disturbed and less disturbable. I return to this important aspect of REBT in Chapter 9.

8

What's the Worst that Could Happen?

I briefly mentioned, in Chapter 5, your imagining one of the worst possible things that could ever happen to you and preparing to deal with this possibility. Let me return to this possibility actually happening and to your dealing in detail with it.

Accepting the Worst Possibilities That Could Actually Happen To You

The worst thing that could ever happen to us is not very likely to happen. But it could. You could discover that you are dying of AIDS or cancer, or that one of your loved ones is in this condition. Or even that the end of the world is in sight, or that some other "terrible" event is about to occur. How could you deal with *this* Adversity?

Let me briefly summarize one of my supervision cases that I described in my book for therapists, *Better, Deeper, and More Enduring Brief Therapy*. Gail, a therapist at our psychological clinic at the Albert Ellis Institute in New York City, was working with Roberta, who was terrified that she might get AIDS from petting even though she and her lover were fully clothed. Roberta also considered handshaking "very dangerous," and was constantly panicked. Gail finally convinced Roberta that AIDS could hardly be caught through petting with her clothes on.

Roberta became less panicked and risked petting with a very safe man, who kept all his clothes on during their petting. When Roberta saw that this kind of restricted petting was quite enjoyable, she became less fearful, and was about to terminate therapy.

Gail and I agreed that this was good progress for Roberta after only 12 REBT sessions. I pointed out, however, that

Roberta was still squeamish about shaking hands with people and was exaggerating any slight aches with which she was afflicted. A stomach ache surely meant that she had cancer.

So I suggested that the next time Gail had a client like Roberta, she go for the elegant solution, and help her see that the probability of her getting a deadly disease was low — indeed very low — but that if she did get it, death would still not be *awful.* Why was it not awful? Because it wasn't 100% bad — she could always die younger and more painfully. And it wasn't *so* bad that it *absolutely should not* ever transpire. No matter *how* bad it was, it *should* be that bad — because that's the way it *was*: very bad!

Gail agreed that Roberta's severe anxiety would probably best relieved if she experimented with the elegant solution that I presented. The next session, she tried to convince Roberta that nothing was awful, including death. She showed her that death, to the best of our knowledge, is exactly the same state as people are in before they are conceived: Zero. No pain, no hassles, no worries: Nothing. Why, therefore, upset yourself about it, when you will ultimately face it anyway, and when worrying about it may well cause you — until the age of 95! — needless pain?

During the session in which Gail presented this argument, Roberta refused to buy it. She acknowledged that death itself might not be so horrible, but that dying painfully might well be. She thought about it more after the session and saw that Gail was almost certainly right. Death itself was nothing to worry about too much; and even dying would normally be pretty quick and painless.

After Roberta came to this conclusion, she was less afraid than ever of contracting a sexual or other disease, began to take more risks, and during her last therapy session thanked Gail for helping her conquer her anxiety. "Now that you've helped me think this thing through," she said, "and even see my death as very *undesirable* but still not *awful,* I feel really freed up. I'll still take precautions against the *realistic* risks of a sexually transmitted disease. And I'm sure I'll have *some* worries for the rest of my life. But not that many and not that severe!"

When Roberta arrived at this more elegant solution to her life-long panics and phobias, her delight in getting there was only rivaled by Gail's pleasure in helping her become so worry-free.

The advantage of your taking the "*Suppose-the-worst-thing-does-actually-happen*" approach is that it not only tends to end your awfulizing about relatively minor "disasters" but about major ones as well. For if you can see that even the worst possibility, if it does occur, is *only* highly frustrating and *not* totally bad, you may thereafter resist making yourself disturbed about practically anything. You can still be *concerned* but not *horrified* about exceptionally bad Adversities.

If you adopt this solution to feeling frantic, you will also stop exaggerating the probability of "dire" things actually happening and will make yourself more emotionally hardy. Thus, Harry was afraid to go to a baseball game for fear that a baseball would fly into the stand in which he was sitting, hit him in the eye, and blind him for life. When he finally accepted the fact that even if this did happen he would suffer but could still survive and lead a happy life, he was able to see that he could choose a safe position to sit in the stands, that he could catch or ward off any ball that was coming his way, and that there really was a very low probability of his bring struck and blinded. He then fearlessly went to many ballgames.

Like the clients I have just described, you can accept the reality that you have no control over what we call "fate" and over many accidents that may happen. If you frantically think that you *have to* control all dangerous events, you still cannot do so, and even if you manage to partly control them, you greatly limit your freedom and your life. Thus, if you avoid "dangerous" airplane flights, you may still be killed in a car crash; and you limit how far and how often you can travel. If you "safely" stay in your apartment, you may still get trapped in a fire. No matter how you restrict yourself, you may fall victim to some germ or other hazard. Tough! But you do not fully control your destiny.

If you accept the uncontrollability of the universe, you will greatly reduce your anxiety about dangers. Once you acknowledge the heavy restrictions you have to place on yourself to keep yourself "thoroughly safe," you will probably see that this kind of "security" is hardly worth it. Also, of course, even your most profound worrying hardly makes you perfectly safe. Life, to some extent, *is* dangerous. If you fully accept this, you will worry a heck of a lot less about its "horrible" dangers and disadvantages. When you are reasonably cautious and vigilant, but still accept the hazards of living, you will give yourself a much greater chance to enjoy whatever life you still have. As Michael Abrams and I have shown in *How to Cope With A Fatal Illness*, people who actually know that they are soon to die can still choose the option of enjoying themselves while they are still living.

Lewis Thomas, the famous physician and writer, did this for several years after he knew that he was afflicted with a rare fatal disease. So did Arthur Ashe, who contracted AIDS from a blood transfusion, and who lived heroically with it. Magic Johnson and Anatole Broyard also handled fatal diseases very well. So did many other less famous individuals, including Warren Johnson, an REBT professor and psychotherapist, who wrote a fine book, *So Desperate the Fight.* Your philosophy of accepting real dangers can help you at times be distinctly uncomfortable but still definitely enjoying.

Do I, as an 85-year-old who has had insulin-dependent diabetes since the age of 40, use REBT on myself? I sure do! When I realize that some of the worst possible things — such as gangrene of the feet or total blindness — could fairly easily happen to me, I quickly convince myself, "Too bad! Tough! That would still not be the end of the world. No, it *wouldn't* be awful or terrible. Only very frustrating and annoying!"

Do I really believe this? Yes, and I got it mostly from philosophy, not psychology.

I adopted the hobby of reading and writing about philosophy, at the age of 16, I concentrated on the philosophy of happiness, and soon figured out that as long as I — and anyone else — was alive and not in too much physical pain, we could always find *something* enjoyable to do even if we were sick, alone, despised by other people, or otherwise deprived of our usual pleasures.

I even figured out, when I was in my twenties, that if I were marooned on a desert island, with nothing to read, nobody to talk to, no radio for listening to music, and no writing materials, I could still write an epic poem in my head, remember most of it if I were ever rescued, and thereby give myself some enjoyment. No matter what, I would still stubbornly refuse to be miserable — as long as I was alive and not in too much physical pain.

REBT gives everyone a similar solution to the problem of human Adversity. It teaches that only constant physical pain may possibly — not always — make your existence worthless. Otherwise, you can find *something* absorbing and worth living for.

What about your being blind and/or crippled? What about your being confined to bed or a wheelchair? What about your being alone and friendless?

No matter! Well, at least it doesn't matter *that much*. Yes, it certainly does *matter* if you are sorely deprived of many or most of your usual enjoyments. It really does. But as long as your restrictions are not total, you can still find *something* to enjoyably live for: music, art, reading, writing, collecting stamps, knitting, gardening, talking on the phone, helping other people. Yes, something that *you* pick, that *you* like, that *you* really feel good about. Yes, in spite of the things you can't do and relish. Yes, in spite of life's blasted limitations!

So don't give up. Don't think that it is hopeless. You can accept social reality (and perhaps injustice) and nonetheless make yourself only *healthily* sorry and disappointed instead of *unhealthily* depressed, terrified, and horrified. Very difficult, yes. But still not impossible. You can almost always find some degree of real, personal enjoyment. If you strongly *believe* that you can!

Once again: work to understand that if some of the worst things happen, you don't have to feel misery and horror. Great trouble and difficulty, yes. Awfulness and terror, no. This is the REBT message that you can firmly believe — and use!

Profound Anti-Whining Philosophies

In 1955, shortly after I created REBT and had vigorously used it with a number of my clients, I was surprised and almost shocked to see that their disturbances, if they and I honestly faced it, often actually consisted of whining. Just that? Well, maybe not just that but largely that.

This became even clearer to me when I saw that the dozen Irrational Beliefs (IB's) that I included in my paper, "Rational Psychotherapy," could be summarized under three major headings: "I must perform well and win approval or else I am an inadequate person!" (2) "Other people must treat me kindly and fairly — or else they are utterly rotten!" and (3) "Conditions must be the way I want them to be or else the world is impossibly bad!" If you strongly hold one, two, or three of these notions you frequently whine and scream about Adversities and make yourself highly anxious and depressed.

If you think about it, you can see that all three of these irrational Beliefs are arrogant forms of whining: "If I don't do as well as I *absolutely must*, I'm a worthless, pitiful person! — Whine, whine!" "If you don't treat me as well as you *absolutely should*, you're a contemptible person for being so rotten to poor woeful me! — Whine, whine!" "If the conditions of my life are not totally good, as they *completely must* be, the world's a really horrible place for poor pathetic me! — Whine, whine, whine!"

If you have any of these godlike demands, fully acknowledge your whining. Don't, of course, put yourself down for your self-pity. Instead, tackle it and help yourself to acquire an anti-moaning philosophy. How? Work along these lines:

1. Acknowledge that you are choosing, are responsible for your self-pitying and complaining. People may be doing you in and conditions may truly be unfair. But nobody *makes you* whine about this. Nobody but *you.*

2. Work at seeing how deadly your bitching and complaining are: Self-defeating. Two-year-oldish. Unattractive. Ulcer- and high-blood pressure-creating. Leading to life-restricting copouts. Certainly not helping you to perform better, to induce others to treat you more fairly, or to change poor environmental conditions.

Jon was sexually abused by his older brother, Tom, when he was a child. He was physically and verbally lambasted by his father, ignored by his mother and called "stupid" and "impossible" because of his learning disability. At the age of ten he was sent to a foster home when his family was declared by the court to be unfit to raise him. Although he worked hard to overcome his reading disability, he didn't have the time or money to finish a four-year college. He did earn an associate degree and became a mental health assistant, rather than the psychologist he wanted to be. Until the age of 27, Jon was often severely depressed about his unkind and unfair fate, and pitied himself greatly for not being able to achieve more. He complained a great deal about the treatment he had received from his brother and father.

Jon had a few psychotherapy sessions during his adolescence, was turned on to REBT by his therapist, and studied it avidly on his own. He first stopped obsessing about the poor treatment he had received during his early life, forgave his father, brother, and mother, and was able to have mildly positive relationships with them. He fully accepted them as fallible humans, tried to help them learn some REBT, and accepted the grim reality that they had no intention of working to help themselves and to lead more constructive lives. While accepting them, he saw that his former bitching and complaining about how they had treated him made him feel "holier-than-thou" temporarily, and covered up his own feelings of inadequacy. He was particularly putting himself down for not somehow finishing college and going on to graduate work in psychology. He finally acknowledged that he had some good economic reasons for failing to finish and therefore was not "stupid" for having picked a para-professional career.

Going beyond this, Jon also acknowledged that he had some low frustration tolerance (LFT), and perhaps even inherited some of the short-range hedonistic tendencies of his family members. At first, he criticized himself severely for this shortcoming, but worked at gaining unconditional self-acceptance (USA) until he really was able to accept his own part in his failings and not cover them up by blaming others.

Jon made what he called a "breakthrough" about his whining, and explained it in one of his final sessions: "From the first time I started reading about REBT, in *A Guide to Rational Living*, I realized that I had low frustration tolerance and that I was still whining about the way I was treated as a child. So I started working on this kind of whining, and within several months I improved considerably. I see what you mean by our human biological tendency to upset ourselves. I still occasionally fall back to whining about poor conditions that are foisted upon me, and feel some real self-pity. But not for very long! I soon see what I'm doing and I stop it.

"I recently saw that *I was covering up some of my own self-downing by whining* about what others were unfairly doing to me. So I started working against this. Then I suddenly realized that putting myself down was also a form of whining. I was saying to myself, 'I *shouldn't* be so pitifully weak. I *should* fight my way through, and still get a graduate degree in psychology. I'm a weakling because I gave in to the economic and other odds against me.'

"So now I'm beginning to stop that crap. I now fully accept myself with my weaknesses. And as I do so, I see much more clearly that I'm not a poor pitiful me. I'm a fallible human, all right — just like all other humans. My weakness is evident, but I'm not a weak, foolish person.

"Best of all, perhaps, I now have a strong anti-whining outlook. I keep suspecting my whining, looking for it, and disputing it. I don't always succeed, but I definitely do it less. Whenever something arises that I could whine about — like my recent bout of the flu — I note my tendency to complain, stop it, and get on with my life. I save lots of time and energy this way. Both my low frustration tolerance and my intolerance of myself for having weaknesses only occasionally arise. When they do, I sock them! That's really energizing!"

Jon's good results with his anti-whining campaign aren't always achieved by clients and readers. Many report that they quickly discover their whining and nip it in the bud. But some of them still easily return to it. REBT says that if you see how often you whine, see how handicapping it is, and keep working to reduce it, you can stop damning yourself, others, and the world. Still, you often may whine, both before and after experiencing Adversities. Indeed, your after-the-fact whining often becomes your before-the-fact outlook. And vice versa! Acquiring an anti-whining philosophy eventually makes you less upset and less upsettable.

Uprooting I-Can't-Ism

In spite of your inborn and acquired tendency to face problems and mend difficulties, you are also born and reared to avoid changing your destructive habits. One of your most self-sabotaging tendencies may be *I-can't-ism.*

Typically, you may select a desirable goal — such as playing the piano well or overcoming one of your emotional problems — and you try a few times but fail to achieve it. You then may irrationally conclude, "See! I'll *never* make it. I can't!" Some people don't even try. All they do is think about trying, and on the strength (really the *weakness*) of that thinking, they conclude, "I can't."

I-can't-ism of this sort particularly ruins therapy. As I often tell my difficult customers (DC's), "As soon as you say and really believe, 'I *can't* change,' you'll make it almost impossible for you to do so. When you strongly say that you *can't*, you won't try too hard to change, will find ways to sabotage yourself — and then you actually won't change. Indeed, we can say that you then have made yourself *unable* to change. Not necessarily because you *really* can't, but because you *believe* you can't. That's the unkindest cut — self-cut — of all!"

I-can't-isms really suck. They may not be the worst thing in the world for your disturbances. But they also may be! Although they won't always make you fail, they certainly help. Look at your own results when you resort to I-can't-ism. Don't you quickly stop yourself from going on? Don't they interfere with your succeeding? Well?

How can you overcome I-can't-ism? Not very easily! Because it is probably a natural and often time-saving result of trying and failing. When you strongly want to do something and you fail at it, you usually judge and decide whether to continue at it.

This is particularly true because you just about always have several alternatives.

Dana, for example, wanted to succeed as an actress, but despite her good looks and her dramatic talents, she only got a few minor and short-lived roles. Why? Mainly because she usually wasn't the type that the auditioners were looking for; and even when she was, ten or twenty other candidates looked as good for the role as she.

Dana was also quite bright and had a talent for designing clothes. So her dilemma was: "Shall I continue to get many rejections in acting, and perhaps never make it in a big way? Or shall I try designing and have a better chance?"

When I first saw her for therapy she was quite depressed about not getting acting jobs. She had concluded, "I *can't* get what I want. I'll *never* make it as an actress. What's the use? I might as well give up." But she was confused, because she also felt, "It would be *awful* if I gave up, because I like acting more than anything else in the world and I *must* make it in that field!"

I saw Dana for a few months and encouraged her to read my book with Bill Knaus, *Overcoming Procrastination*, and to listen to several REBT tapes. Dana began to Dispute her Irrational Beliefs that she *absolutely must* be an outstanding actress, *must not* get rejected so often, and *couldn't possibly* succeed. She initially got over the first two of these self-defeating notions and felt much better. But she insisted that because the odds of steadily getting acting jobs were slim, she definitely *could not* get them. So she procrastinated about going for any auditions, and began to put all her energies into becoming a clothes designer.

I persisted in showing Dana that she could stop jumping from, "It's *quite difficult* for me to get a good acting role," to "I absolutely *can't* get one." I also helped her to Dispute her jump from, "My acting rejections are so awful that I *can't ever* feel disappointed rather than severely depressed about them. Therefore, I *can't* suffer this pain and *must* give up on being an actress!"

Dana actively forced herself to act against her depressing Irrational Beliefs, and to still go for auditions even though she hated to do so. She was able to give up her feeling of depression and instead only feel sorry and disappointed about her rejections. Her audition networking enabled her to get some jobs designing clothes for theatrical and film productions. Her income from this source helped her to keep looking for acting roles, and she eventually became a fairly steady performer *as well as* an up-and-coming designer!

Seven Steps To Beating I-Can't-Ism

If you suffer from I-can't-ism, how can you lick it? In several ways:

1. Show yourself, as mentioned above, that you naturally and easily tend to jump from, "It is *difficult* for me to get what I want, and I have *tried and failed* to do so several times," to "I *can't* ever get what I want." Your conclusion here just doesn't follow your initial observation. Difficult means, at most, just that: hard to achieve. It rarely means impossible.

2. Show yourself that your very Belief, "I can't accomplish this! I'll never be able to do so!" is often a self-fulfilling prophecy that will encourage you prematurely to give up and to "prove" that you can't. Don't act like many people who derive grim satisfaction from "successfully" predicting their failures!

3. Realize that many goals — such as getting your first novel immediately accepted by a leading publisher — have a low probability of success. But your reduced chances practically never sink to zero. Yes, there are some things you really *can't* do — such as be perfect. But you *can* change your thinking, your feeling, and your actions. If you *think* you can!

4. Demonstrate to yourself that you have accomplished difficult and "impossible" things before — and so have many other people. See that all things sooner or later change, including mountains. You have made some remarkable turnarounds in the past. People who swear, "I can't change" often actually do. Many individuals have made almost 180-degree changes. Business people, for example, have become priests or nuns; priests and nuns have turned to business. Distinct change *is* possible!

5. Change requires a significant amount of thought and effort. When you energetically push to modify yourself, you have a good chance at succeeding. No certainty — but a heck of a good chance!

6. Watch out if you are saying, "I *will* change," in order to stop yourself from going through the hard work of *actually* changing. Will power, including the will power to change yourself, includes several points, as I noted in Chapter 5: Your *decision* to change, your *determination* to act on that decision, your gaining the *knowledge* of how you can change, and your steadily *acting* on that knowledge. Your saying, to yourself and

others, "I will change," may easily be a mere expression of will, with no *power* to back it up. It may also be a rationalization to avoid changing. "I will change" is only an empty promise if you don't put work behind it.

7. Get back to the two main levels of changing yourself.

On Level 1, you needlessly upset yourself first, by mainly commanding that you, others, and world conditions *must not* be as bad as they are. Because you are the commander, you can also make yourself into a non-commander. You are born and reared to easily upset yourself, but you also have the constructive tendency of *un*upsetting yourself. So you *can* put this latter tendency to work!

On Level 2, you frequently disturb yourself about your disturbances; and that, too, is your choice. So you can *choose* to do otherwise: to refuse to upset yourself about your upsetness.

In both these cases, you'd better strongly convince yourself that you *can* change, that you have the ability and power to do so, and that when you fall back you can improve once again.

This last acknowledgment is very important if you want to make yourself less disturbable. No matter how many times you have undisturbed yourself, you can and probably will at times fall back to thinking, feeling, and acting destructively. When that happens, you recognize that you managed to unupset yourself before by using REBT; and therefore, it is most probable that you can do so again. What's more, you can keep doing so for the rest of your life. You may fall back considerably, but your ability to change yourself remains. The fact that you did improve before, is good evidence that you can do so again. You've changed yourself previously; that proves that you are inherently self-alterable!

You are also a creature of habit. Once you learn how to drive a car or speak a foreign language fairly well, you normally retain the habit of doing so. Even when you stop driving or stop speaking another language for awhile, you rarely lose all your ability to do these things, and you can bring yourself up to your old level again with a certain amount of practice. As the old saying goes: "Once you learn to ride a bicycle..."

This is also true with making yourself less disturbed. Once you reduce your feelings of panic, depression, rage, and self-hatred, and practice doing this over a period of time, you tend to get in the habit of feeling less upset. You then are able to fairly easily reduce your self-defeating feelings and behaviors. You know how you previously did so, and you have confidence that you can do so again — just as you have confidence that you can competently driving a car and speak a foreign language.

You can also figure out what you can do to avoid bringing on less emotional pain and how to decrease it if you experience it again. You thereby can make yourself *remarkably less disturbable*. You don't *have to* learn prevention in this manner; but you definitely can learn it. Knowing in advance — by the theory outlined in this book — that you can learn to reduce your proneness to disturbance, you can consciously take special pains to teach yourself how.

Preventing Disturbance

Josefina learned REBT mainly by reading my books and listening to our recorded materials and came for a few sessions of psychotherapy to check on her gains and to actualize herself some more. She originally had a dire need for political success to prove that she was popular and therefore really a *good person.* When I first saw her she only liked herself because she was a leading state senator. She also insisted that she have several close friends, because socializing was one of her greatest joys. She felt cut off — "practically a hermit" — when a few of the people she really liked stopped calling her and only saw her when she kept after them to do so. So she had both self-downing and low frustration tolerance in her social relationships.

From reading and listening to REBT materials, Josefina showed herself that she was okay as a person even if she lost her Senate seat, and that she could stand having fewer close friends than she would have liked to have. So she was doing quite well with her dire needs for popularity and for close friendships. She gave up most of her self-downing and her anger at people who showed that they were not her real friends.

Josefina from time to time fell back into her destructive mode: putting herself down for being less popular politically, and feeling angry and self-pitying when her social life was less than she demanded that it be. When that occurred, she quickly was able to look at her irrational demands on herself, on others, and on the world, to actively Dispute these demands, and to change her feeling from unhealthy depression to healthy sorry and regret. Moreover, she kept watching her own progress in overcoming her double neediness, saw that she kept falling back to it, and then used forceful REBT Disputing to relieve her disturbed feelings. She realized that her ways of upsetting herself and her methods of using REBT procedures to undisturb herself again followed a similar pattern, and that she almost automatically resorted to both of these practices.

She then decided to go a little further. Whenever she fell back to her dire need for political popularity and close friendship, and to consequent feelings of depression when they were absent, she reviewed her previous REBT Self-Help Forms and her previous tapes of her own forceful Disputing of her irrational Beliefs. She saw that she only had to slightly revise them and add to them. Thus, she replayed a tape she had made where she vigorously Disputed her Irrational Beliefs, "I can't be *at all* happy with myself when I do poorly in an election" and where she powerfully ended up with, "Crap! Nonsense! Drivel! I can *always* accept myself no matter *how* unpopular I am! I can! I darned-well will!" This got her out of her depression and ultimately made her much less depressible.

Josefina then devised her own *preventive* procedure. Whenever she saw her political or social popularity waning, she realized in advance that she could easily depress herself about this. So she used REBT Self-Help Forms to write out the Irrational Beliefs (IB's) that she most probably would be reinstating if she made herself depressed, and she went over them *in advance of actually becoming depressed.* When she did this, she found, first, that she made herself depressed less often about her impending "doom." Second, because she was less disturbed, she was able to consider the practical aspects of the situation in which she was involved and act more sensibly to achieve political success and interpersonal closeness. Even when she was not able to resolve these practical problems, however, she found that she less often felt depressed and self-downing.

Josefina was quite effective in figuring out how to prevent herself from sliding back to disturbed feelings. Following her lead, I have used it after with a number of my other clients. I get them to look for what Josefina consciously found on her own: To see that they do upset and unupset themselves and can obviously keep doing so. Then I help them see that they can predict, in advance, that they sometimes will disturb themselves again, and that they can use the same methods they have previously used to undisturb themselves. By noting this, they look for emotional problems before they become severe and they work at preventing them.

You too can do this if you are determined to work at reducing your unhealthy reactions. First, you work at reducing them *when you actually feel disturbed.* Second, like Josefina, you *review in advance* your self-upsetting and unupsetting patterns. You then work at *preventing* upsetness, or nipping it in the bud while it is not too severe. You won't, of course, be able to eliminate all your emotional difficulties. Even when you do prevent some, you probably will fall back again. But you can consciously make yourself less disturbable if you keep working along the lines described in the previous two paragraphs.

Consider Moderation, Balance, And Openendedness

Sometimes extremes are pretty good. If you are extremely happy about a relationship, or even about not having one, that may be fine — for you. If you are greatly devoted to an activity, a vocation, a business, a hobby, or a cause, that may also do you a lot of good. Even if you are unusually cautious and inhibited, as long as you really don't mind restricting yourself, you may still be content.

So not all extreme views and actions are bad or self-defeating. But many are. Severe sadness, regret, and displeasure may interfere with your life, even though these feelings may be healthy and appropriate after you have suffered a grave loss. But extreme anxiety, depression, self-hatred, rage, and self-pity will rarely help you, will tend to make you cope less adequately with troublesome problems, and may leave you incapacitated and listless.

Again, many one-sided actions make you less enjoying. If you only work, work, work, you will miss out on other satisfactions — including, often, intimate relationships. If you compulsively try to relate, relate, relate, you may fail to gain job satisfactions, money, and fame. Because your time, energy, and talents are limited, extreme devotion to one project or cause almost always restricts you from other enjoyments.

So, ironically, does extreme preoccupation with optimism. Pessimism, as Martin Seligman and other psychologists have shown, has its real dangers, and can lead to depression, despair, and inertia. On the other hand, Pollyannaism or over-optimism, as Shelly Taylor and her co-workers have pointed out, can unrealistically help some people who otherwise think they *can't stand* grim reality. Pollyannaism — the view that everything will happen for the best — also frequently ends up with feeling disillusionment and horror. For, obviously, everything *won't* happen for the best; and into every life a heck of a lot of rain frequently falls. We don't want it, but it darned-well happens.

Pollyannaism or unrealistic optimism also can stop practical concern and caution. When you are unemployed, if you are "sure" that a marvelous job *will* come along soon, what practical steps will you take to find one? If you are "certain" that your mate will love you dearly, just because you're you, no matter how you treat him or her — well, lots of luck with that unrealistic view!

As Aristotle pointed out over two thousand years ago, there usually is a mean between two extremes. And if you take it, it rarely gets you into serious trouble. Consider the findings of Robert Schwartz and other psychologists, that people who much of the time have positive or optimistic thoughts (about 65%) *and* negative or pessimistic thoughts (about 35%) thoughts lead a fairly balanced, and hence less disturbed life.

This is also the view of REBT. *Realism* is a fairly good Aristotelian mean between extreme pessism and extreme optimism. To be realistic is to fully acknowledge the undesirable aspects of life, to view them as "bad" or "obnoxious," and to motivate yourself to try to change them. When you can't modify them or escape from them, you then feel frustrated, sorry, or disappointed — which are not great feelings but are still healthy.

REBT teaches you not to *overreact* either way to Adversities. You do not Pollyannaishly ignore them, deny them, nor insist that they are really good, much less feel elated about them. But you also do not exaggerate, catastrophize, or awfulize about them and thereby sink yourself into panic, depression, or despair. Because you remain realistic and concerned, you don't minimize *or* maximize Adversities. You keep yourself less disturbed about them and cope with them more effectively. Which is one of the main goals of moderation and balance: To create fewer "horrors" in life, and to cope more successfully and less anxiously with those difficulties that inevitably will occur.

Moderation and balance also give a fuller and more rounded view of experiencing, and thereby increase your choices. If you see "togetherness" as the best goal for you, striving for it may well add to your life. If you view it as *the one and only* goal, you will ignore its restrictions, frustrations, and limitations. You may also ignore the advantages of solitude and self-sufficiency. A *balanced* view encourages you to see both sides — or all sides — of togetherness and aloneness, work and play, art and science. It lets you explore new horizons, take untrodden pathways, make yourself less one-sided and rigid.

The REBT view, remember, sees disturbance largely as rigidity, dogma, absolutism, and musturbation. Moderation and balance counter this black-and-white thinking by adding many grays — and brighter colors! REBT is postmodern in that it accepts no ultimate, unquestionable, absolute view of "reality" but sees it as an ever-changing, newly interpreted process. It favors relativism, subjectivity, and provisional conclusions about humans and the universe. But with some "facts" added!

This concept of balance between extremes may not be entirely your thing. You may be accustomed to a more conservative and orthodox life view, and such an outlook may work well for you. But consider its other side — its restrictions and limitations. Try to be open-minded enough to see the disadvantages of both absolutism and extreme postmodernism. Yes, both! Need you be stuck in strict inflexibility or unstructured relativism? Or can you healthily consider some of the grays?

Forget About Magical Solutions

Perhaps there is real magic in the world. Perhaps you can quickly and easily tap into some form of Cosmic Consciousness, some Higher Power, some Secret of It All, some Mystical Intuition, or some Transpersonal Meaning that will make you totally free from all troubles and miseries and present you with a fully self-actualized and ecstatic life.

Perhaps. But if I were you, I wouldn't count on it. Whatever your beliefs in magic, shamanism, past life therapy, higher consciousness, mysticism, cultism, or any other form of miracle cures, don't let them interfere with your *own* self-help efforts.

No, you most likely don't have, and won't find, any magical solutions to your emotional and behavioral problems. And you don't *need* any. Insight is often easy to come by. But changing can be very hard! The more magic you seek, the less you will do what you *can* do: Work your head off to change! So believe what you believe about Magic Helpers and Miraculous Gurus with perfect solutions. But work to implement the old saying, "God helps those who help themselves!"

As I noted previously, even wrong Beliefs may sometimes help you. Believing that God will answer all your prayers or your faith in spiritual revelations from a Saint or Guru who died several centuries ago, may enable you to push yourself and thus improve your life. Maybe!

Beliefs in magical "solutions," however, will usually sabotage the hard and persistent work at self-changing that you require to make yourself less disturbable. The conviction that you can reduce your upsetability, and the effort to back up this conviction, almost always includes the view that *you*, and not some magical force or power, can really do this. Trust in magic will hardly keep your powder dry — nor your will power strong!

Accept the Challenge In Adversities

Many bad things have some good in them. Difficult problems are interesting to try to solve. Losing a love relationship gives you the opportunity to find other, different, and sometimes more satisfying intimacies. Being fired from a job may motivate you to improve your skills, look for a better job, or prepare for a new vocation.

If you look at it sensibly, almost any hardship gives you a *challenge* to make yourself feel healthy negative feelings — such as sorrow, regret, frustration, and annoyance — which can help you cope with and change this Adversity. It gives you the challenge of *refusing* to experience unhealthy, self-sabotaging feelings of panic, depression, rage, self-loathing, and self-pity.

Adversity is not exactly great. But it can provide real benefits — if you view it properly! This is one of the main points you can put on your agenda of getting better, staying better, and finally achieving automatic emotional health.

Look at this fascinating problem in terms of the will power described in Chapter 5. How do you gain the will power to uproot your disturbed thoughts, feelings, and actions — and to keep most of them from arising again?

Not very easily! This is a real challenge — and one that you can use considerable will *and* power to effect. Let's review our discussion of will power. You can apply these steps to accepting the challenge of Adversities and striving to make yourself less disturbable:

1. *Decide* to work very hard to achieve the elegant solution to your emotional problems — to make yourself considerably less disturbed now and distinctly less disturb*able* in the future. *Accept* Adversities you can't change, and *choose* to be less upsettable about them.

2. *Determine* to act on your decision to work hard and make yourself less disturbed and less disturb*able*.

3. *Acquire knowledge* of what to do, and what not to do, to carry out your will, your decision. Carefully study the methods described in this book and in other writings, materials, talks, courses, workshops, intensives, and (perhaps) individual and group psychotherapy sessions. That's right: *study*.

4. Start *acting* on your determination and your knowledge. Work at finding, Disputing, and changing your Irrational Beliefs (IB's) and replacing them with self-helping Rational Beliefs (RB's) or Effective New Philosophies (E's). Work at altering your unhealthy negative feelings about Adversities (A's) — such as severe anxiety, depression, and rage — to healthy negative feelings — such as sorrow, regret, and frustration. Work at modifying your self-defeating behavioral Consequences (C's) — such as compulsions and phobias — to helpful behavioral C's — such as freedom from compulsions and phobias, such as flexibility, curiosity, and adventurousness.

5. Keep steadily and persistently *deciding* to change your disturbed thoughts, feelings, and actions, *determining* to change, *acquiring knowledge* about how you can change, and *acting, acting, acting* to make yourself change.

6. If — as well may happen — you fall back to your disturbed thinking, feeling, and behaving, once again *decide* to minimize your disturbances, *review your knowledge* of how to change your ways, *make yourself determined* to act on your knowledge, and *force yourself to implement your decision and your determination.* No matter how difficult you find this thought and action to be? Yes.

7. Work hard at achieving three related goals: One: making yourself less disturbed *right now.* Two: *keeping* yourself less self-defeating and socially destructive. Three: *working persistently and strongly* at these two goals, undesperately striving to accept the fascinating challenge of making yourself considerably less disturbable. (But not totally undisturbable!)

With this kind of will, you may well make it. If you give determination and action — that is, *power* — to your will.

9

Thinking Ways to Make Yourself Less Disturbable

I have been describing REBT methods you can use to make yourself less disturbed and remarkably less disturbable. In the next four chapters I shall illustrate a number of other thinking, feeling, and action-oriented techniques. You can especially use these to undisturb yourself whenever unfortunate Adversities (A's) happen to you (yes, even when *you* help make them happen!).

The methods I am about to describe are the bread and butter (or margarine!) of effective therapy, and are commonly used in REBT and several other popular methods. They are backed by much clinical and experimental evidence. I have personally used aspects of them for almost a half century — often with fine results. However, *they are not good for all people all of the time.* Occasionally, some of them may be harmful. So use them — paradoxically! — with enthusiasm and with some caution.

Will the self-therapy methods in the next four chapters really help you? Quite likely they will. Will they make you distinctly less disturb*able*? Sometimes. Especially if you use them forcefully and persistently. However, I shall also point out some of their limitations — and, hopefully, encourage you to try the more elegant procedures that I advocate throughout this book.

Once again! — effective therapy is usually complex. What works for you may not work for your brother or sister. What works today may no longer be effective tomorrow. So you'll find here a whole smorgasbord of REBT methods that are tried and true — for some people some of the time. In this and the next chapter (10) I present a number of useful thinking or cognitive techniques followed by a chapter (11) of emotional, evocative and a chapter

(12) of behavioral methods. Consider them, experiment with them, test them out with your most interesting subject — you!

Rational Emotive Behavior Therapy, as I have already noted, is the first of the major cognitive-behavioral and multimodal therapies. From its start, REBT has pointed out that your thoughts, your feelings, and your actions all are interrelated: When you think about something that is important to you, you have emotions and behaviors. When you feel mad, sad, or glad you have thoughts and actions. When you put yourself in action, you have thoughts and feelings. All three go together and affect each other, though they are not exactly the same, and though we often speak of them as if each has its own separate existence.

When you feel and act disturbedly, you also have thoughts, feelings, and behaviors about your upsetness. You observe and think about them: "This is an unpleasant feeling I am having. What shall I do about it?" You emote about them: "I feel sad and depressed about doing worse than I am able to do at work." You act in regard to them: "I'll go for therapy or take some medication now that I feel so depressed."

REBT therefore says: When you are self-defeating, you'd better investigate your thinking, feeling, and behaving, then use a number of cognitive, emotive, and action methods to overcome or reduce these problems.

In this and the next chapter, I shall show you some of the main cognitive or thinking methods you can employ whenever you observe that you are functioning below your potential level of work, love, and play. Even a single one of these methods may help you to relieve your disturbance and to lead a more enjoyable life. Using several of them will usually help even more, because some of them overlap with and reinforce each other.

First, let's get to the regular cognitive methods of REBT, which are also used by a number of other therapies, that have produced good results over the years — some of them over the centuries.

Finding Your Self-Defeating, Irrational Beliefs

As I previously noted, and as you can now review in the first four chapters of this book, whenever you are disturbed, the chances are high that you are consciously and/or unconsciously thinking some irrational or self-sabotaging Beliefs (at point B). You are taking some of your normal desires, goals, or preferences and making them into *absolutistic shoulds, oughts, musts*. The three major musts that you and the rest of the human race tend to invent are: first, ego-musts: "I *absolutely must* perform well and be approved for what I do or else I am worthless!" Second, relationship musts: "Other people *completely should* and *must* act considerately, kindly, and fairly to me or else they are no darned good!" Third, environmental musts: "The conditions under which I live *ought at all times* to be the way I would like them to be, or else life sucks, the world is *awful,* and I *can't stand* it!

Assume, then, that you have one, two, or three of these godlike commands, and acknowledge that your *demands,* and not merely your *preferences,* for success, good relationships, and comfort make you disturbed when they are not fulfilled. Face it: *You mainly disturb yourself.* Events are often bad enough, and cause you real losses and hassles. But when you — yes, you — take life's misfortunes *too* seriously, you thereby create much more unnecessary havoc than you would otherwise experience. You are not a fool or a slob for doing so, but whenever you feel quite disturbed, you are very probably thinking, feeling, and acting idiotically and slobbishly.

Disputing Your Self-Defeating, Irrational Beliefs

As I noted in the first four chapters of this book, because your grandiose, musturbatory Beliefs are largely self-adopted or self-created, you can change them — fortunately. You easily and naturally tend to believe them. Others encourage you to believe them. You have practiced believing and acting on them on many occasions. And, if they still affect you, you still believe them now. But you also have the power to disbelieve them. You are a born self-harmer; but you are also a born self-helper. You can therefore use your problem-solving ability to undo your destructive tendencies. If you *choose* to do so! If you *work* at doing so.

Therefore: review the methods that I outlined in Chapters 2, 3, and 4 to realistically, logically, and pragmatically Dispute your self-defeating musts.

Realistic Disputing: "Where is the evidence that I *must* always succeed at this important project? How does failing at it make me a *thoroughly worthless individual*?"

Logical Disputing: "Because I have often treated you nicely and fairly, *how does it follow* that you must now treat me equally well?"

Pragmatic or Practical Disputing: "If I keep believing that I *must* win the love and approval of every person that I care for, where will this belief get me?

Keep finding your musts and demands, and actively, vigorously Disputing them, until you firmly see that they never really hold water. Once you turn almost any of your *preferences* into arrogant *musts*, you tend to create derivative Irrational Beliefs (IB's) that increase your woes — such as *awfulizing, I can't-stand-it-itis, damning of yourself and others,* and *overgeneralizations.* You can usually find these derivative IB's easily and quickly and you can actively Dispute them again and again. For example:

Disputing awfulizing: "It is certainly bad if I fail at an important project, but is it really awful and terrible? Is it *one-hundred percent* bad? It is *more than* bad? Is it 'badder' than it *absolutely should be?*"

Disputing I-can't-stand-it-itis: "Can I really *not stand* losing so-and-so's love? Will this loss *kill* me? Does losing it truly mean that I can't be happy *at all, now or forever?*"

Disputing damning oneself and others: "While I acted badly in lying to my friend, does that action make me a thoroughly *rotten, damnable person?* If my acts are wrong, do they make me a hopeless, complete wrongdoer? Granted that I behaved badly, do I deserve *no joy whatsoever* for the rest of my life?" "If I make a mistake, does that make *me* a mistake or a loser?"

Disputing overgeneralizations: "Because I failed miserably at this important test, does this prove that I shall *always* fail at any other test that I take?" "Though I have procrastinated on this project for a long time, how does that show that I can *never* do it and can *never* quickly finish any other projects that I undertake?"

Disputing rationalizing: "Suppose I claim that I really don't care *at all* if I get rejected by so-and-so. Does it help me lead a good life to pretend that succeeding at this project is *quite unimportant?*"

If you firmly and consistently find your disturbance-creating philosophies and actively Dispute them, you will not be entirely undisturbed for the rest of your life, nor will you be endlessly happy. But you will be a hell of a lot better off!

Constructing and Using Rational Coping Self-Statements

Rational coping self-statements — sometimes called positive thinking — was invented thousands of years ago, and can be read in *Proverbs* in the Bible and, in the *Analects* of Confucius, in *The Manual* of Epictetus, and in a number of other ancient writings. In modern times, positive thinking was particularly promoted by Emile Coué, the originator of autosuggestion, who clearly realized that if you tell yourself positive sentences — especially, his famous saying, "Day by day in every way I am getting better and better!" — you will frequently help yourself to overcome your misery and to function more effectively. In more recent years, positive thinking has been promoted, with or without giving credit to the ancient philosophers and to Coué — by Norman Vincent Peale, Napoleon Hill, Dale Carnegie, Maxwell Maltz, and a host of other writers of self-help books.

Does positive thinking work? Unquestionably — at times. People have invented slogans that have at times helped to cure themselves of various kinds of ills. You can, too, if you use some well-chosen positive self-statements.

Watch it, however! Emile Coué, the most popular therapist in the world in the 1920s, went out of business because his positive self-suggestions were often Pollyannaish and unrealistic. Who truly gets better day by day in every way? Not very many! Who actually, as Napoleon Hill pushes you to do, just thinks and grows rich? Hardly anyone!

Moreover, if you devoutly push yourself with outlandish positive thinking, you can easily soon make yourself disillusioned and then give up on practically all self-help procedures. One of my 50-year-old clients, Sidney, read everything that Norman Vincent Peale ever wrote, went to many of his sermons at Marble Collegiate Church in New York, and turned many of his friends onto trusting completely in God and in the Reverend Peale, to cure themselves of all their ills. When some of these friends, in spite of their vigorous positive thinking, wound up in the mental hospital, and when Sidney had to turn to massive doses of tranquilizers to keep himself going, he became disillusioned with all forms of psychotherapy, and advised his friends and relatives against it. But after seeing me work with volunteers at my regular Friday Night Workshop on REBT at the Albert Ellis Institute in New York, and by realizing that people could Dispute their Irrational Beliefs and come up with their own effective coping self-statements, Sidney gave up his crusade against therapy, went for some REBT sessions himself, and was able to cut down on the heavy medication that he had been taking.

The REBT method of creating rational coping statements differs from other methods of positive thinking because it starts with your Disputing (D) some of your Irrational Beliefs (IB's), coming up with Effective New Philosophies (E's) and then using your new ideas as the basis for formulating your coping statements. For example, suppose at point A, Adversity, you get a poor performance rating at work, instead of the good one that you thought you would get. You may then think, feel, and act as follows:

A (Adversity): Receiving poor performance rating.

RB (Rational Beliefs): "I hate getting this kind of rating. How annoying! I'd better do something to get a better one next time."

C (Healthy Negative Consequences): Feeling sorry and disappointed.

IB (Irrational Beliefs): "I *must not* get this kind of rating. How horrible! I'm a really poor worker and a rotten person for doing this badly!"

C (Unhealthy Consequences): Feeling anxious and depressed.

D (Disputing): "Why must I not get this kind of poor performance rating? Is it really *horrible* to get it? How does it make me a really poor worker and a rotten person?"

E (Effective New Philosophy): "Obviously, there's no reason why I *must not* get such a poor rating, though it would be much better if I didn't. It's highly unfortunate that I got it, but it's not *awful* or *horrible*. Only very inconvenient! I'm certainly not a really poor worker, because I often do well at work. And even if I were incompetent at work, I can never be a *rotten person*, but only a *person who* is now incompetent in this area and who can change and make myself more competent."

If you think things through in this manner, and actually arrive at E, your Effective New Philosophy, you can then rephrase it and make several rational coping statements out of it. For example:

1. "It's highly undesirable to get a poor rating at work but there's no reason why I *must* never get one."

2. "Many inconvenient things exist in my life, such as getting a poor rating at work, but none of them is *horrible* or *awful*."

3. "Doing poorly for a while never makes me a poor, incompetent worker."

4. "Getting low performance ratings does not make me a rotten person. People who do poorly are not bad people, but they are only people who are now doing worse than they would like to do."

5. "I don't like getting a poor rating but I can live with it and still make my life reasonably happy. Even if I get fired, my life doesn't have to be utterly miserable."

If you will look at these statements, you will see that they follow from your Disputing your irrational Beliefs. Your Effective

New Philosophies (E's), and your rational coping statements are not arbitrary. They are not taken from others, and are not unrealistic and Pollyannaish. They are realistic, logical, and likely to help you. They tend to change your Irrational to Rational Beliefs, rather than to cover them up, sweep them under the rug, and avoid dealing with them. If you are wise, you will not merely parrot these rational coping statements, and thus only lightly believe them. You will also think about them, keep proving to yourself that they are accurate and helpful, and thereby strengthen your Belief in them.

You will also note that your rational coping statements, as listed above, are philosophical as well as realistic. Thus Statements 1, 3, and 4 are realistic or empirical, in that they state some of the facts of social reality. Statements 2 and 5 are also realistic but go somewhat beyond that and include a philosophy that is likely to help you live happily rather than miserably.

Other coping statements that you create may be realistic but not philosophical, such as:

1. "When I got this poor rating I thought I was hopelessly bad at this kind of work and could never improve, but now that I think about it, I am pretty sure that I can do better in the future."

2. "I thought that my supervisor was prejudiced against me when she gave me this bad job rating but now I see that she probably wasn't, and that maybe I really performed worse than I thought I was performing. If I push myself to change my ways, I most likely can do much better."

These realistic self-statements may be accurate and helpful but they still cover up two major self-defeating philosophies. If you tell yourself that you can do better on the job in the future, you may still not be facing and changing your irrational ideas. Such as, "If I never can do better, I am unquestionably an inferior, inadequate person!"

By telling yourself that your supervisor was prejudiced against you and that you really did better than she thought you did and that therefore you deserve a better job rating, you may temporarily feel good about what happened. But you may still think, first, that if your supervisor was not prejudiced against you and if you really did poorly, you are an incompetent person. Second, you may conclude, that if she is prejudiced, she is a rotten assessor and therefore is a total no-goodnik. In these instances, your coping statements again temporarily work to help you feel better but they don't change your underlying philosophy of damning yourself when you do poorly and cursing other people when they do not treat you well.

Once again, don't repeat what happened in the case of the great number of people who followed Emile Coué and consequently believed that "day by day in every way they could do better and better." Watch out for creating Pollyannaish statements like these:

- "Yes, I guess my job rating shows that I did rather poorly this time. But I just didn't use the great ability that I have and that I can use next time. I'm sure I can be the finest worker that this firm ever had and I definitely will be!"
- "I guess my poor rating shows that I was overconfident and thought that I was doing better than I actually was doing. But I obviously have more ability to work well than anyone else in my department, and I'm certain that I'll show my supervisor how great I am next time!"
- "Yes, I did poorly this time. But that's because this kind of work is far below me. I should be doing something much more complicated, like cost analysis or even brain surgery. To hell with this job I am doing! I'm going to go to graduate school and be the finest cost analyst or brain surgeon who ever existed. I'll show them what I can do!"

These kinds of unrealistic, grandiose, and Pollyannaish views may help you to feel better, get over your depression, and perhaps accomplish more than you are now doing. But, again, such statements may cover up an irrational underlying philosophy, which demands that you *must* do well, *prove* how good a person you are, gain more approval than other people, and easily get what you want in life. So Dispute (D) your Irrational Beliefs, come up with New Effective Philosophies (E's), make them into rational coping statements — but review these statements to see how much good, and also how much harm they may do you. Coping statements like, "I can do better. I'm sure I can!" are optimistic and sometimes effective. But they also can have lots of flaws and hazards.

Positive Imagery and Visualization

Several ancient thinkers clearly saw, and Emile Coué advocated in modern times, that if you use positive visualization you can

help yourself perform better and feel good about your performances. Psychological experiments have backed up this theory.
If people practice *imagining* themselves hitting a tennis ball well
or speaking effectively in public, their *visualized* practice will
often help them almost as much as *real* practice at doing these
acts. Try this and see for yourself.

If, for example, you are afraid of doing poorly at job
interviews, imagine yourself having a difficult interview, fielding
the questions well, impressing the interviewer, and getting a very
favorable reception. If you vividly and repeatedly imagine
yourself behaving competently, you will tend to develop a sense
of self-efficacy — that you *can* handle the situation. Instead of
thinking, "I can't really do this well. I'm no good at job
interviews" (thoughts which leave you feeling inadequate), you
will tend instead to begin to say to yourself, "This is tough, but I
can do it. I think I've got what it takes!" You'll be gaining what
REBT calls "achievement confidence." With such confidence, as
many experiments by Albert Bandura and his students have
shown, you are much more likely to do well in difficult tasks
than if you lack confidence or harbor a philosophy of self-doubt.

Practicing an activity — job interview, speech, golf-swing —
in your head is sometimes fairly close to practicing it in vivo, in
real life. Practicing a speech imaginatively, for example, may give
you some excellent ideas for it, may lead you to create some
clever phrases, and may help you develop arguments that you
would not otherwise devise.

One downside of positive imagery is that it may discourage
you from changing your horror of failing, or sometimes actually
increase it. Suppose, for example, you are anxious about
meeting someone socially. Your anxiety almost always stems
from an Irrational Belief, such as: "I *absolutely must* do quite
well in this encounter. I simply *have to* impress this person and
make her think that I'm one of the greatest socializers she ever
met. It would be *terrible* if I fell on my face and she concluded
that I was a jerk. I'd die if that happened!"

Being so determined to impress this other person, you keep
imagining yourself talking to her, having brilliant ideas, coming
up with clever statements, and notably impressing her. You even
imagine overhearing her tell someone else, after you've met her,
what a bright and great person you are. All this kind of positive
visualization makes you feel good because it bolsters your idea,
"You know, I really *can* do well in my social affairs. I'm sure that

I really can. Therefore, I'll welcome the chance to get into social relationships and do my best to succeed at them."

Well and good. Thinking this way, you may actually approach social relationships and may start doing pretty well. However, you are still underlyingly (and often openly) anxious. You are socializing, true, but you may be still believing the same philosophy that you had before: that you *must* do well, that it would be *terrible* if you didn't, and that you'd die if you were seen as a "social jerk." In fact, your self-image that you are acting well — coming up with brilliant statements, impressing the person you want to impress — may actually reinforce your dire need to perform well and to have her approval.

What's more, even when your positive visualization helps you socialize, it practically never stops you from thinking, "Well it's great that I'm socializing so well right *now*. But suppose I fail *later*? Suppose I run out of fine things to say and am stopped dead in my tracks? Suppose the person I am talking to now thinks that I'm okay but later finds out that I really am a dud? Suppose she then sees how foolish I really am and begins to despise me? How really awful that would be! I would sink into the ground and never be able to show my face in public!"

So even when positive imagery gives you a temporary lift, it is almost always a Pyrrhic victory that doesn't change your basic outlook, and keeps you as anxious as ever. For it may cover up, and does not really improve, your basic self-downing philosophy.

Therefore: use positive visualization and thinking, if you will. But remember that they may lead to denial instead of problem-solving. Instead, look for and Dispute the underlying demands and musts that you have about succeeding and winning other people's approval. Identify these demands you probably still have, and actively Dispute them and give them up. Then your positive thinking and visualizations may really work — and not sabotage you later!

Using Referenting or Cost-Benefit Analysis

Referenting is an REBT term for referring to both advantages and disadvantages of a behavior, instead of taking a one-sided view that may favor your harmful addiction to it. Thus, whenever you keep acting against your own best interests, and particularly when you remain addicted to behavior that you "know" is self-defeating, you may be focusing upon only its good or helpful aspects, while you are simultaneously ignoring its harmful aspects. You may be telling yourself, "It's *too hard* to change!" or "I *can't* change!"

Suppose, for example, you "know" that drinking, smoking, or gambling is "bad" for you and you keep promising yourself to stop it — but, no, you still continue to indulge in it. Why are you behaving in such a foolish, self-destructive manner? Because, at the time you are indulging in this harmful behavior, you are actively focusing your immediate gratification, and you may be looking away from the harm that you will ultimately obtain. You're concentrating, in other words, on the *advantages*: the pleasure of drinking, smoking, or gambling, and refusing to think about the *disadvantages*: health hazards, turning people off, and other dangers of your addiction.

If so, you had better begin to balance your view by referenting or cost-benefit analysis. Focus upon and connect with the real disadvantages of your indulgent behavior. Sit down and take some amount of time — a week or two, for example — to make a list of the distinct harms of your indulgence. Write down as many disadvantages as you can list for continuing it.

If you are compulsively gambling, for instance, list the main harms of doing so: The amount of time you spend gambling; the money you often lose while doing so; the alienation of your family, friends, and non-gambling associates. Its other distinct disadvantages.

Write down these disadvantages, and then take at least ten minutes every day to think about the harmful effects of your gambling. Deliberately focus on — instead of foolishly distracting yourself from — these disadvantages. Take time — perhaps three or five times every single day — to remind yourself of these costs. Go over them, again and again, until you remember them, keep them well in mind.

At the same time, keep reminding yourself of the advantages of not gambling: the time and money that you save, the longer life you may have, the proof that you *can* exert good discipline, the pleasure and the benefits for your friends and relatives, the good modeling for your children.... .

Take time to make a good list of the benefits of giving up your unwanted habit and the pains of retaining it. Actively think about the items on the two lists that you make, and do not merely parrot them or easily gloss over them. Bring to mind, preferably, real cases of people you know who have suffered from the disadvantages on your list. Discuss these disadvantages with others. Keep adding more to your list, if you at first do not include them. Forcefully go over the hazards of your addiction. See what you are telling yourself to ignore or deny your habits. Dispute any Irrational Beliefs that encourage you to remain addicted. Use some of the behavioral methods described in Chapter 12.

Robert was a compulsive gambler. No, he did not indulge in steady gambling at the casinos in Atlantic City, but several times a year he would take a weekend off and lose a few thousand dollars, which he could ill afford. Even when he was ahead a thousand dollars or more he invariably killed his own chances by convincing himself that luck and skill were with him and that he was going to make a real killing. He became so excited about the prospect of making a bundle that he could hardly think straight and lost most of the skill that he otherwise had at blackjack and poker.

Robert used active Disputing of his Irrational Beliefs to try to stay away from Atlantic City. He often succeeded; but he also went back to the Irrational Beliefs: "My life as an auditor is exceptionally dull and I therefore *need* some excitement. Even though I sometimes lose a good deal of money in a weekend, I don't have any other expensive pursuits, such as collecting antiques, and therefore I'm still ahead of the spending game. Besides, my family doesn't suffer too much from my gambling losses."

Robert at first resisted referenting because he sensed that doing so would stop him from the pleasures that he "really needed" to make his life worth living. When he did a little referenting, he omitted listing some of the main hazards of his gambling; and when he made a good list of these hazards he only went over them infrequently and lightly. Finally, he agreed to the penalty of not going to Atlantic City at all until he had made up a good list of the disadvantages of his gambling. None of the losses that he listed impressed him very much except one: Whenever he gambled and lost a considerable sum, his wife became angry at him and refused to have sex for weeks thereafter. When doing his referenting, he made himself focus on this great disadvantage.

To his surprise, he discovered that it really wasn't the sex that he missed so much — because he was in his mid-fifties and was hardly as erotic as when he had married at 35. But knowing that his wife was incensed about his gambling, that she only spoke to him harshly and omitted all the affection that she normally gave him, and also knowing that their two children sided with his wife and felt that she was rightly angry at him — by focusing on these very unpleasant realities of his family life, he was able to stop going to Atlantic City. Also, he helped bring his gambling under control by organizing a bet-limited poker game every two weeks with some of his friends, in which he managed to break even in almost all of the games he played.

REBT Cognitive Homework

Effective therapy usually shows people what to do in-between sessions, and not merely during their individual or group therapy sessions. In the course of my clients' first few sessions, I usually tell them, "Write down during the week any of your feelings and your behaviors that are troublesome — such as feelings of anxiety and depression, or avoidances of things that you really would like to do. Note the Activating Events or Adversities (A's) that precede these events. You now have A and C of the ABC'S of your disturbed feelings and actions. Then assume that you also have Irrational Beliefs (IB's) that spark your sabotaging yourself at C. Find these IB's — which nearly always include musts and demands. Then actively Dispute them until you arrive at E, your Effective New Philosophy." My clients usually have no trouble doing this, and soon they are quite aware of the ABCDE's of their disturbances.

You can do the same thing, whether or not you are in psychotherapy. First, check your C's to see how you feel and act self-defeatingly. Then observe what usually occurs at point A, just before your disturbed behavior. Find your IB's, forcefully Dispute them (D) and figure out your Effective New Philosophies (E's) (aka Effective Rational Beliefs). Don't hesitate to go over your ABCDE's with friends or relatives, especially if they know some REBT. But even if they don't, you can actually teach them some of the main elements of REBT, so that they can help you and use them on their own problems.

To help write down your ABC's of REBT and to do your Disputing (D) and come up with Effective New Philosophies (E's), Windy Dryden, Jane Walker and I have devised the following *REBT Self-Help Report Form*, which you can regularly use. After awhile, you will know it by heart and will probably be able to do it in your head.

A > Ballet / Not doing whole class
IB > Not good enough
E > Doesn't matter how bad -
only way to get better -
mistakes are chances to figure out

REBT Self-Help Form

A (ACTIVATING EVENTS OR ADVERSITIES)

- Briefly summarize the situation you are disturbed about (what would a camera see?)
- An A can be *internal* or *external, real or imagined.*
- An A can be an event in the *past, present, or future.*

IB's (IRRATIONAL BELIEFS)

To identify IB's, look for:

- DOGMATIC DEMANDS (musts, absolutes, shoulds)
- AWFULIZING (It's awful, terrible, horrible)
- LOW FRUSTRATION TOLERANCE (I can't stand it)
- SELF/OTHER RATING (I'm / he / she is bad, worthless)

D (DISPUTING IB'S)

To dispute ask yourself:

- Where is holding this belief getting me? Is it *helpful* or *self-defeating?*
- Where is the evidence to support the existence of my irrational belief? Is it *consistent with social reality?* Is my belief *logical?* Does it follow from my preferences?
- Is it really *awful* (as bad as it could be?)
- Can I really not *stand it?*

C (CONSEQUENCES)

Major unhealthy negative **emotions:**

Major self-defeating **behaviors:**

Unhealthy negative emotions include:
- Anxiety
- Depression
- Shame/Embarrassment
- Rage
- Hurt
- Low Frustration Tolerance
- Jealousy
- Guilt

E (EFFECTIVE NEW PHILOSOPHIES)

To think more rationally, strive for:

- NON-DOGMATIC PREFERENCES (wishes, wants, desires)
- EVALUATING BADNESS (it's bad, unfortunate)
- HIGH FRUSTRATION TOLERANCE (I don't like it, but I can stand it)
- NOT GLOBALLY RATING SELF OR OTHERS (I—and others—are fallible human beings)

E (EFFECTIVE EMOTIONS & BEHAVIORS)

New healthy **negative emotions:**

New constructive **behaviors:**

Healthy negative emotions include:
- Disappointment
- Concern
- Annoyance
- Sadness
- Regret
- Frustration

© Windy Dryden & Jane Walker 1992. Revised by Albert Ellis. 1996.

REBT Self-Help Form

A (ACTIVATING EVENTS OR ADVERSITIES)

- Briefly summarize the situation you are disturbed about (what would a camera see?)
- An A can be *internal* or *external*, *real* or *imagined*.
- An A can be an event in the *past*, *present*, or *future*.

IB's (IRRATIONAL BELIEFS)

To identify IB's, look for:

- DOGMATIC DEMANDS (musts, absolutes, shoulds)
- AWFULIZING (It's awful, terrible, horrible)
- LOW FRUSTRATION TOLERANCE (I can't stand it)
- SELF/OTHER RATING (I'm / he / she is bad, worthless)

D (DISPUTING IB'S)

To dispute ask yourself:

- Where is holding this belief getting me? Is it *helpful* or *self-defeating*?
- Where is the evidence to support the existence of my irrational belief? Is it *consistent with social reality*?
- Is my belief *logical*? Does it follow from my preferences?
- Is it really *awful* (as bad as it could be?)
- Can I really not *stand it*?

C (CONSEQUENCES)

Major unhealthy negative **emotions**:

Major self-defeating **behaviors**:

Unhealthy negative emotions include:

- Anxiety
- Depression
- Shame/Embarrassment
- Rage
- Hurt
- Low Frustration Tolerance
- Jealousy
- Guilt

E (EFFECTIVE NEW PHILOSOPHIES)

To think more rationally, strive for:

- NON-DOGMATIC PREFERENCES (wishes, wants, desires)
- EVALUATING BADNESS (it's bad, unfortunate)
- HIGH FRUSTRATION TOLERANCE (I don't like it, but I can stand it)
- NOT GLOBALLY RATING SELF OR OTHERS (I—and others—are fallible human beings)

E (EFFECTIVE EMOTIONS & BEHAVIORS)

New healthy **negative emotions**:

New constructive **behaviors**:

Healthy negative emotions include:

- Disappointment
- Concern
- Annoyance
- Sadness
- Regret
- Frustration

However, you'll often find it useful to write down your ABCDE's, so that you can check and review them later. Frequently, moreover, you will repeat the same basic Consequences and needlessly upset yourself. So by referring to some of your previous Self Help Forms you can quickly see how you have Disputed your IB's before and what Effective New Philosophies (Rational Beliefs) you have devised.

The Use of REBT and Other Cognitive-Behavioral Educational Materials

As I have previously mentioned, once I began using REBT with my regular clients and with members of the public, I realized that people could use written, recorded, and other educational materials to help themselves with their therapy and with their self-therapy. For REBT itself is unusually educational, during and outside of therapy sessions. Its principles can clearly be explained, as I am explaining them in this book, and they can then be used by most people who want to apply them to themselves. In turn, those who learn the principles can teach them to others as I shall discuss below.

Scores of pamphlets, booklets, and books have been written that present REBT clearly and effectively. At the psychological clinic of the Albert Ellis Institute in New York, we recommend that our clients read a group of pamphlets published by the Institute that we give them at their first session. These include, "The Nature of Disturbed Marital Interaction," "REBT Diminishes Much of The Human Ego," and "Achieving Self-Actualization."

We also recommend that our therapy clients read some of the main REBT and CBT books for the public, such as my books, *How to Stubbornly Refuse to Make Yourself Miserable About Anything — Yes Anything!; A Guide to Rational Living; A Guide to Personal Happiness*. Other books that we frequently recommend include: Paul Hauck's, *Overcoming the Rating Game*, and my own *Overcoming Procrastination; How To Control Your Anger Before It Controls You; The Albert Ellis Reader;* and *Optimal Aging: Getting Over Getting Older.* These are but a few of the REBT pamphlets and books that you can use. A good many other items as well as audio-visual materials, are starred in the References section at the back of this book, and a list of new materials can be obtained from the Albert Ellis Institute, 45 East 65th Street, New York, NY 10021-6593, (212) 535-0822, Fax (212) 249-3582. The Institute's free catalogue also includes a list of the current talks and workshops that it gives on REBT.

Most people find these materials, as well as talks and workshops on REBT and cognitive behavior therapy, quite useful. My clients, in particular, once they have some REBT sessions, find that reviewing our literature and the audio-visual material brings to mind some of the methods they are currently neglecting, as well as some they may never have used before. Even if you have not had any Rational Emotive Behavior Therapy sessions, you will probably find these materials quite helpful.

Teaching REBT to Your Friends and Relatives

Soon after I started using REBT with my clients, I found that a number of them began to teach it to their friends, relatives, and business associates. As noted above, they had little trouble doing so, as long as they understood it fairly well themselves. Second, some of the people they taught benefited by it right away. Others at first resisted but then saw how helpful it was to my clients, and then started to use it themselves.

The more my clients taught REBT to others, the more they often helped themselves. This is what famed educator John Dewey pointed out almost a century ago: We learn to do something well by teaching it to others. This is especially true of REBT. When you show others that they do not, as they erroneously believe, merely *get upset* by Adversities in their lives, but that they also choose, consciously and unconsciously, *to upset themselves*, you keep drilling this idea into your own head and heart. As you show these others their Irrational Beliefs and how to Dispute them, you tend to see your own IB's more clearly and to improve at Disputing them.

This is one of the main reasons I started to do REBT group therapy in 1959. I saw that in group, my clients had an excellent opportunity to see other members' Irrational Beliefs and to Dispute them. Moreover, I could supervise their working with the others, point out what IB's they rightly and wrongly observed, and show them how to improve their Disputing. Those who actively participated in group learned how to uncover and Dispute their own IBs more successfully. The group also was highly educational, because members saw other members struggling with similar problems and could see how frequently some of the others' IB's matched their own. They learned how others' ways of Disputing could be used on their own disturbances. This was effective modeling!

If you can get together a group of your own friends to learn REBT and use it together, fine. But even without this you can use it with almost anyone who will talk to you about their problems. Once you start teaching REBT to even one person, he or she can in turn use it with you, can check your own IB's and Disputings, and you both can see how well you are using it with yourself.

Rosalie was severely depressed about the breakup of her relationship with Ronald two years before, and at times even thought of suicide to end her misery. After I had seen her for eight weeks, she realized that it wasn't merely the loss of the relationship that was upsetting, but her putting herself down severely for having lost her temper with Ronnie. She was sure that she could never overcome her childish temper tantrums, that she would not be able to sustain a good relationship with anyone, and that she was consequently an unlovable, worthless person.

In the course of her REBT sessions, along with her reading and listening to REBT materials, Rosalie learned that her fits of temper resulted from her own childishly demanding that people *absolutely must not* balk her strong desires — especially her dire need to be loved by them — and that they were "ungrateful bastards" when they thwarted her. She also saw that her "need" for constant shows of affection was unrealistic and illogical. It was a "necessity" only because she *defined* it as such.

Rosalie saw that she had both abysmal low frustration tolerance and severe feelings of unworthiness, and that they stemmed not from her failing to win enough affection but from her impossible demands on herself and her love partners. She worked hard at keeping her strong preferences while giving up her dogmatic demands for love. With this change, she made herself undepressed and returned to the dating scene, which she had abandoned before she came to therapy.

As Rosalie discussed her problems with a few of her women friends and showed them how she was now handling them with REBT, she found that almost all her friends were similarly afflicted. In addition to their healthy desires to love and be loved, they frequently lapsed into thinking that they *absolutely had* to fulfill these desires. Showing their neediness frequently turned off their lovers; and even when their relationships were going well, they remained anxious by thinking, "I must *continue* to be loved, or else I am an unlovable, worthless individual!"

Rosalie clearly saw her own errors as she helped her friends to see that, like her, they were foolishly making their healthy preferences for love into dire necessities, and thereby defeating themselves. Some of her women friends, with her help and by reading REBT literature, significantly improved. One of them stopped plaguing her boyfriend, as Rosalie had previously plagued her own lover, and began cementing a relationship that she had been seriously disrupting. Another friend continued her present relationship but made herself less anxious whenever her boyfriend got preoccupied with his work and neglected her. All told, Rosalie's friends benefited considerably from her help with REBT principles, and she herself learned them more solidly. As frequently happens in cases like this, Rosalie decided that she so greatly enjoyed helping others with REBT that she enrolled in graduate school to become a clinical social worker.

Modeling

As Albert Bandura and other psychologists have shown, children and adults learn a great deal from modeling themselves after others, and you may have mirrored from relatives and friends some of your own self-defeating absolutistic musts. Your family members, your teachers, your culture, the mass media — all these have shown you ways to damn yourself, fight with others, whine about your misfortune, and otherwise upset yourself. Not that you are yourself untalented in this respect. You can easily make up your own crazy rules and your own rigid insistences about following some of these rules. But you are also a suggestible and gullible person — like all humans — and you have no trouble in modeling yourself after others, in helpful and unhelpful ways.

Suzie, for example, was a born and bred copycat. She changed her ways of dress with every new fashion that became the rage for awhile. She copied the hair, makeup, and perfumes of the most popular members of her social group. Her rules of conduct were not her own, but were very much like those of the people she admired at school and in her conservative Long Island neighborhood. To make things worse, she sabotaged her own individuality by insisting that her own and her in-group's personal rules were indubitably "right" and "proper" and that anyone who ignored them, including she, was an outcast and a slob.

Suzie came to see me because of her chronic anxiety, which broke out whenever she broke one of the "right" social laws, or when others thought that she was breaking one. Then, as you might well suspect, she made herself extremely anxious about others' seeing her extreme anxiety.

I used several of the usual methods of REBT with Suzie, especially identifying and Disputing her main Irrational Beliefs: "Improper social conduct is terrible, never to be forgiven, and always to be avoided at all costs!" "If I stand out from my crowd like a sore thumb, all the good people despise me and they are right to do so: I am a social misfit and the lowest of the low on the community totem pole!"

After several months of REBT — which she first fought strenuously but finally adopted because five previous years of psychotherapy had not worked — Suzie became moderately independent and stopped kowtowing to the most conservative members of her social group. She dressed and made herself up in her own tasteful way, stopped drinking to conform to her peer group's tastes, and even talked enthusiastically about her liberal reading to some of her conventional friends. She also acquired several less-conventional Manhattan friends to replace some of the "Long Island types" that she no longer enjoyed.

Suzie's anxiety distinctly decreased — especially her panic about appearing anxious. She still maintained most of her close family ties — although she was sometimes ashamed to let her stuffy relatives know that she occasionally dated and had sex with more than one man at a time. She pretended to go with only one of her lovers, brought him steadily to family gatherings, and never hinted that she had a steady relationship with another man, too — one who was quite unconventional and who would never be, in her relative's eyes, a "suitable candidate" for marriage.

Suzie felt quite uncomfortable about her dishonesty, though she had stopped putting herself down for her "poor" behavior. To get over her discomfort, she did several REBT shame-attacking exercises in the course of which she told her family about some of her "outlandish" actions. She managed to feel unashamed when she let them know, for example, that she had stopped attending the Catholic church and instead had joined a Buddhist group.

To go even beyond this extent of risking family disapproval, Suzie read the works of several Zen Buddhists, as well as such Christian nonconformists as Henry David Thoreau and Bronson

Alcott, who shamelessly broke a number of social rules. By modeling herself after these nonconformists, Suzie was able to distinguish herself even more from her family's expectations, and to become her own person. She finally let just about everyone, within and outside her family, know about her sex activities and she felt comfortable doing so. She was proud of the fact that she was also able to convince a couple of her oldest, most conservative woman friends to lead less conventional sex and love lives.

I am not, of course, advising you to adopt unconventional ways like Suzie and some of her friends did. You are free to keep whatever liberal or conservative customs you want to keep. But if you really desire to do anything unusual — in any direction — you can usually find a number of people in real life and in biographies who went against the grain and were not embarrassed about doing so. You can help yourself by modeling yourself after their "shamelessness."

Avoiding Overgeneralized Language

As Alfred Korzybski pointed out in 1933 in his unusual book, *Science and Sanity*, and as several other authorities have also indicated, we humans are a uniquely language-producing animal. Without the use of language, including self-statements, we would not be able to do well in our thinking, in thinking about thinking, and in thinking about thinking about our thinking.

Language is indeed a boon to the human race — in many ways. But hardly always. Our tendency to invent and to keep revising our language includes its own dangers. As Korzybski showed, we easily overgeneralize when we speak to ourselves and others. Thus, when using the *is* of identity, we accurately note, "I acted foolishly by not studying for this important test," and then we overgeneralize: "Therefore I *am* a fool!" We may even go beyond this and say, "Because I acted foolishly, and therefore *am* now a fool, this makes me a rotten, undeserving person who *always* acts badly and who doesn't deserve to enjoy my life."

If you think about these statements, you will see that you may often tend to make them to yourself and to others, and that they are obviously inaccurate. That you acted foolishly may be true because your goal, let us say, was to pass the test, and you probably would have passed it by studying. But you chose to avoid studying and thereby sabotaged your own goal. Because you acted against your own interests, you can legitimately say, "I behaved foolishly." This helpfully brings to your attention what you did, and what you can do differently the next time you take a test.

Moreover, in REBT terms, if you only observe that you acted foolishly about your test-taking procedure, you will probably conclude that because your behavior was unfortunate, you prefer not to repeat it. You will then make yourself feel sorry and disappointed with this behavior, and your negative feelings will, once again, be healthy or self-helping. If you make yourself feel happy or neutral about your destructive behavior, you will tend to keep repeating it; while if you make yourself feel sorry and disappointed about it, you will tend to avoid it in the future.

How about your statement, "For acting foolishly about my test-taking procedure, I am a fool!" Well, how about it? Obviously, it is inaccurate, because the conclusion, "I am a fool!" implies that you only and always — or at least much of the time — act foolishly. Actually, you probably do many things, perhaps most things, pretty well and unfoolishly. So you are errantly overgeneralizing. You are also a victim of what Korzbyski called the *is* of identity. For your statement, "I am a fool!" in some ways makes your foolish *behavior* equal *you*, your entire substance and being. What rot! You do thousands of other things besides test-taking; even in taking tests, you sometimes study for and take them well; and, as in this particular instance, you sometimes do not. So you are obviously not, in all probability, "a foolish test-taker," and you are almost certainly not "a foolish person."

What *are* you? Well, that in itself may be a silly question, because you do so many different things that you *are* not any one of them. If anything, you are a *person who* acts well and badly; who this time acted badly or foolishly; and who next time can act differently and better. Unless you only do one thing in life, and always do it exactly the same way, you just about never *are* what you *do*. Yes, you *do* what you do; and because you have some measure of choice or will, you can be said to be *responsible* for doing and/or not doing it. But you engage in a great many behaviors, and you cannot be totally labeled for *being* good or bad in any of them. Even if you were consistently bad in any of them, you cannot accurately be labeled a *bad person*. As psychologist Stevan Nielsen (personal communication) has noted, when you label yourself as a *bad individual* you harshly *define* what a person who behaves adequately *should* supposedly be. You *arbitrarily invent* the essence of human adequacy — *make it up* for yourself.

So your ability to use the verb *is* or any other form of the verb *to be* and to designate your whole self, or entire being, as "I *am*, this" or "I *am* that" is very tricky. You had better monitor and curb it. David Bourland, Jr., one of the leading members of the International Society for General Semantics (a group that follows Korzbyski's teachings), has devised a form of English called *E-prime*, which avoids all uses of the verb *to be* and whose usage is therefore less likely to lead to the kind of overgeneralizing, to the "*is* of identity," that we are discussing. Using E-prime will not change all your crooked thinking into straight thinking about yourself and others, but at times it may be helpful.

Back to musturbation. As noted above, when you say, "I acted foolishly about my test-taking," you tend to feel sorry and disappointed, and these healthy negative feelings help you to correct this procedure in the future. But when you add, "And therefore I am a fool," or "Therefore I am a rotten person for acting so foolishly and being a fool," you tend to change your preference for helpful behavior into an absolutistic must. The statement, "I am a fool!" implies that "fool" is your identity as a person, and that you will *always* act foolishly. If you believe it, you will get quite bad results! If so, you will again tend to raise your preference for not acting badly into a dogmatic demand: "Because acting foolishly will make me a fool, who will then always keep acting foolishly, I *absolutely must not* act that way! It's awful when I do! My acting foolishly makes me a damnable, undeserving person!"

Now where are you? Nowhere! Your prediction that you always have to keep acting foolishly may easily become a self-fulfilling prophecy and actually make you keep acting that way. You will also imply that you are *incapable* of acting unfoolishly, so you might as well give up any attempt to do so. You will further imply that others will see what a fool you are, will despise you, and will hardly ever give you a chance to act well. Some of your onlookers may even deliberately sabotage you and your attempts to try to do better. You may also imply — if you think that fate and the universe are personally interested in you and object to your being a fool — that people and fate will see you as an undeserving clod, will make sure you don't ever succeed and act well, and may actually punish you and ban you from having the opportunity to act properly and get good results for the rest of your life.

Now look at the mess you have created!

Of course, all these dire results may not follow from labeling yourself, quite inaccurately, as a "good person" or a "rotten person." But they may result! So be careful: Set up important goals and values and do your best to achieve them — mainly because you strongly *want* to do so. And when you fail to do so — and even when you fail because you fairly obviously did not follow correct procedures, such as studying for a test when you want to pass it — designate only your *actions* as bad, foolish, or ineffective. Don't — foolishly! — label *you*, your *whole self*, your *personhood*, as bad. Realize that, like all humans, you are truly fallible.

No, and don't label your entire *self*, if you want to be accurate, as "good" or "deserving." Labeling yourself as a good person or a deserving person will probably get you better results than labeling yourself as a bad person or an undeserving person, but both labels are really inaccurate. Because — as George Kelly and others have shown — humans tend to think in constructs or categories that are *dichotomous*, whenever you think of something as good, you will almost always contrast it with something you think is bad. So whenever you think of yourself as being a *good person* you will tend to believe that you also can be a *bad person*. Quite dangerous!

Take the elegant REBT position on personhood: only rate or measure your thoughts, feelings, and actions by whether they fulfill your goals and purposes; don't rate your entire self, being, substance, essence, or personhood at all. Watch your language, especially your overgeneralized language. Observe, and be very skeptical about, self-statements like these:

- "Because I failed this time, and perhaps several times, I'll *always* fail."
- "Because I failed at this important task, I *am* a Failure with a capital F."
- "Because I could have done better, and I failed to do as well as I could have done, I am not only responsible for my poor behavior, but I *am* also a poor, inadequate, undeserving person."
- "Because other people act shabbily to me, they *make* me angry at them."
- "Because the world in which I live has a good many unfortunate or rotten conditions, it truly *is* a rotten world!"

These and similar labels and overgeneralizations won't always make you disturbed. But they will often get you into needless trouble with yourself — and with other people, who may resent your labeling *them* by some of their poor *actions*. Labeling and overgeneralizing are not the root of all human evil. But the root of a lot of it!

So interrupt your overgeneralizing. Especially quit identifying your whole self with some of your behaviors. You may never completely stop doing this kind of exaggerated generalizing, but you can cut it down considerably! You'll find it is one of the most important tools you can use to make yourself healthy, happy, and less disturbable.

10

More Thinking Ways

Problem Solving, Insight, Spirituality, & Self-Esteem

Practical Problem Solving

A good deal of psychotherapy, including that which often takes place in REBT, consists of practical problem solving. Obviously, if you solve your life problems, and if you *don't* demand that you have a perfect or best possible solution for them, you will not feel very disturbed. However, you and other people often feel emotionally upset when you are faced with some kind of a life problem, are having difficulty solving it, and conclude that there is no good solution to it. The Activating Events or Adversities (A's) in your life are against your interests. At point B, your Belief System, you often think irrationally about not having good solutions to them. And at C (Consequence) you needlessly upset yourself about A. Your upsetness then *interferes* with your ability to manage the practical problems you face.

It is good to work at solving practical problems, and effective therapy will help you do this work. But if you *only* or *mainly* do this, you hardly reduce your emotional upsetness. Your practical problems may soon arise again, and you will still tend to be easily upsettable when you have no great solution for them. So in REBT, we recommend working at *reducing your disturbances* before and while you work on your practical problems. In particular, avoid telling yourself that you *absolutely must* always come up with the best possible solutions to these problems.

Terry worked as a management consultant and was quite good at this kind of work. He was often able to show large corporations what they were doing inefficiently and how to make their procedures more efficient. He liked problem solving, and tended to run his own life well, too. His ex-wife was constantly after him to provide more money for their two young children, so he figured out methods of pacifying her, making more money, budgeting the income that he had, and spending his resources carefully. He even calculated that dating was often expensive, and that therefore he would only date those women who required his spending little on them. These methods worked pretty well; he met all his bills and was not too worried about doing so.

When Terry's firm downsized and only employed him on a part-time basis, his income suddenly dropped and he began to deplete his savings. He began to worry incessantly that he might have to find another position, that his children would hate him for giving his ex-wife less money, and that the women he dated would look down on him for not being financially secure.

Terry's concern about having enough money was a healthy negative feeling, because it helped him make plans for earning more money or living adequately on his reduced income. But Terry was *over*concerned, obsessed about money, constantly worried even when he was paying his bills, and felt like an inadequate person for being "poor." He often spent sleepless nights and made frantic money-saving decisions that got him into difficulties with his ex-wife and his present womanfriend.

REBT helped Terry to keep his healthy financial concerns while giving up his extreme overconcern — including his prediction that he might end up on welfare. I showed him that he indeed had monetary problems, but even if he never succeeded at solving them, his worth as an individual was not involved. He also read my book with Patricia Hunter, *Why Am I Always Broke?*, and saw that poor financial condition never makes you an inadequate *person*.

Terry finally concluded, "You know, I may never find a great solution to my financial problems, because in my industry things may never return to normal. If so, that will be quite bad, financially. But, at the worst I'll just have to spend less, give less support to my children, and put up with their displeasure. If they won't understand, they won't understand. And if my girlfriend puts me down for having little money that will just prove that she's not the one for me. Even if she sees me as a lesser person, I certainly don't have to agree with her!"

When he reached this conclusion, Terry was still financially strapped but much less anxious and self-downing. He still was good at practical problem solving. But he now held the self-helping philosophy that the *situation* was bad when he wasn't doing well financially, but that *he* was not a bad or inept person.

By all means, then, do your best to solve your practical problems. Use methods that are widely employed in business, industry, and management, and that have been promoted by psychologists and educators like Donald Meichenbaum and Gerald Spivack and Merna Shure. Some of the techniques that they recommend include the following:

- Analyze important problems, particularly those that you tend to upset yourself about.
- Avoid taking on too many problems that have deadlines and that require quick solutions.
- Try to figure out the best answers for your problems but don't make "best" into "only." Be prepared for alternative — and sometimes "worse" — solutions as well.
- Try a number of possible answers, both in your head and sometimes in practice, even when, at first blush, only one of them really seems to be suitable.
- Check your solutions, again in your head but preferably in practice, to see whether they produce the kind of results that you want.
- Assume that it is possible for you to find good answers for your problems but do not assume that you *have to* discover great ones.
- Help yourself to set realistic goals by stating your problems clearly and working at some possible solutions to them.
- Try to generate a good many potential solutions so that you have a better choice among them.
- When you feel stress or anxiety about your problems try to think how other people might deal with them without creating so much anxiety.
- Evaluate the pros and cons for each of the answers you consider and rank them for their possible good results.
- Try to rehearse some of your possible strategies and behaviors before actually trying them out. As you work on them, try to imagine possible better answers and check out these possibilities in your head.

- Expect some failures, sometimes a good many, and do not insist that they must not occur or see yourself as a lesser person if they do occur.
- See that it is good that you tried, and sometimes reward yourself for trying, even when your plans do not work out well.
- Convince yourself that you can still keep going once you are engaged in solving a problem and that there is a good chance that you will finally solve it.
- When you are blocked, see what you are telling yourself to possibly create your blocking. Are you telling yourself that it is *too* difficult to go on? That you will *never* be able to solve the problem? That you will *only* come up with poor results, as you *must* not do? That anything worth doing *absolutely must* be done well?
- Think about and use some encouragements that help you proceed with your problem solving. Consider self-suggestions like, "I really can do this." "I enjoy this kind of problem solving." "Now that I'm doing well, I can most probably do even better." "Even if I don't succeed I can learn a good deal by continuing to try."
- Convince yourself that if the worst happens and you never come up with a good solution to a problem, no disaster will occur and you can still find things to be happy about.
- Try to see the situation, even when you are doing poorly at resolving it, as a real challenge, and sometimes as an exciting challenge. You can almost always help yourself by attempting to solve the problem, by learning even if you don't solve it, and by enjoying the process of trying to find good and better answers. Be prepared to accept yourself fully — to have what REBT calls unconditional self-acceptance (USA) — even when you come up with poor solutions.
- You can also achieve high frustration tolerance: that is, convince yourself that life would be *better* if you solved your problems quite well, but it's not *awful* if you don't. You can still *stand* it, and you can also arrange to have a reasonably happy life when some of your important problems remain unsolved.

Don't forget that working on your emotional problems, which often block your work on your practical problems, is itself a form of problem solving. So keep asking yourself, "How can I solve my emotional problems?" as well as "How can I solve my practical problems?" Both require using your head! The REBT approach is first to look at your emotional blocks and hang-ups, resolve them to some extent, and then go on to deal with practical life problems. But this is hardly an invariant rule. As long as you eventually improve your disturbed emotions, you will be in fairly good shape.

Solution-Focused Techniques

A group of therapists, following the path of Steve deShazer, have recently made solution-focused therapy popular. Even before deShazer, Milton Erickson started to do this kind of therapy in the 1950s, and deShazer has added to Erickson's somewhat unusual techniques. REBT has also advocated many of these methods since the 1950s.

Solution-focused therapy doesn't go at great lengths into your past, as does psychoanalysis. Instead, it tries to show you that you do have natural constructive tendencies, that you have at times used them effectively, and that you can learn by your own experiences to use these methods again in the present.

The solution-focused approach helps you to realize that to a large degree you are born a problem-solver, and that your very life often depends on your having this kind of ability. Solution-focused therapy tells you that you have this self-changing ability, and at times you use it very well. Therefore, when faced with a practical or emotional problem right now, you can remember how you effectively coped with similar problems in the past, and can use or adapt your old solutions to cope again today.

Knowing this, you ask yourself several pertinent questions. Suppose, for example, you are now anxious about failing an important course, and you keep obsessing so much about the "horror" of failing exams that you focus poorly when studying for it, and panic at the thought of taking it. If so, you ask yourself several important questions:

"What did I do about overcoming my anxiety when I was last in a situation like this? What worked for me? Did I mainly force myself to concentrate better despite my anxiety? Did I convince myself that passing this course isn't sacred? What did I do that I can try again?"

Again, ask yourself: "What changes did I make in my studying that were most helpful? What methods of calming myself worked and what did not work in the past? What interrupted my problem, when I had it before, and made me handle it better? What made it worse?"

Once again: "Did I make myself anxious about my anxiety the last time I was in a situation like this? Did I insist that I *must* not be anxious and was no damned good as a person for being anxious? Did I insist that my anxiety was *too hard* to take, that it *shouldn't* exist, and that life was *unbearable* because of it? If I did not down myself for being anxious, how did I avoid doing so? How did I work on my low frustration tolerance about my anxiety when I had it before?"

If you ask yourself questions like these about how you previously solved your anxiety about taking an exam, you will Dispute your awfulizing about it because you stop to think what worked when you formerly viewed this situation as "awful."

Solution-focused therapists would have you focus on a more concise future orientation rather than focus on your past and present problems. You concentrate on behaviors that are not working for you rather than get obsessed with understanding yourself and getting a good diagnosis of what you "are." You try to set up interventions (forced choices) that help you change in one way or another, no matter which choices you take.

Still again: be action-oriented and review the progress and outcomes of your homework assignments. Interrupt well-rehearsed disruptive patterns of thought and behavior.

All these suggestions have value, and overlap with the many thinking, feeling, and action methods that REBT favors. However, solution-focused therapy's outcome orientation may ignore the deeper and elegant methods that I advocate. For example:

- You sometimes cannot remember how you previously solved either your practical or your emotional problems — even when you actually did solve them in the past.
- Were your previous solutions really good ones or just fair ones that merely helped you get by? Obviously, they were not deep, else the same problems would not so easily recur.
- Your previous solutions, because they "worked" to some extent and sometimes gave you some immediate relief, could have actually prevented you from figuring out better and deeper solutions. Left to your own devices, you may have low frustration tolerance that encourages you

to devise and stay with quick and easy solutions rather than more complicated and efficient ones.

- Your solutions may tend to be one-sided. Thus, if you manage to get yourself over your phobia of trains or elevators, you may not go on to overcome many of your other anxieties, and may merely tolerate and live with them.
- Your tendency, as a human, is often to revert to old disturbances once you have partly overcome them. But REBT holds that, if you get to some of your very basic musts and uproot them you will relatively rarely make yourself seriously upset again, and therefore will not have to keep using your "solutions" over and over.
- If you have a distinct personality disorder, solution-focused therapy may ignore the fact that intense and sometimes prolonged therapy may be required, and that anti-depressant or other medication may be useful.

Gerald, for example, was very unhappy in the monogamy-oriented system in which he was reared in the Midwest and that still prevailed in New York City when he moved there at age 25. So, with much trouble, he managed during the next few years to help found a non-monogamous collective in Brooklyn, where about a dozen men, women, children, lived together, shared expenses, and allowed free, and presumably unjealous, exchange of sex partners. For awhile, Gerald was delighted with this arrangement. But he soon found that practically all the commune's members, including himself, brought their neurotic thoughts, feelings, and actions to this new community, and by the time the commune was about to go into its third year, chaos reigned. He himself was exceptionally angry much of the time because some of the group's members promised faithfully to follow agreed-upon rules and then ignored them, lied about following them, and even deliberately sabotaged some of them.

By the time the commune disbanded, Gerald saw that he himself was by no means sufficiently unneurotic to live in it successfully, nor were practically any of the other members. In fact, he decided that the only way such a community could work would be for just about all its members to have a good deal of effective therapy themselves, to ameliorate their tendencies for self-downing, jealousy, anger, and low frustration, tolerance, and then to see if their particular kind of commune could really work.

By all means use some of the methods of solution-focused therapy. If you want to mainly help yourself in the present, and possibly to do so briefly, they may well work. But if you want to make what I keep calling an elegant, profound philosophical and behavioral change, you'd better add to these methods some of the "deeper" ones that I describe throughout this book.

Use Your Strengths, but Avoid Pollyannaism

Milton Erickson and the solution-focused therapists who continue to advance some of his views, showed their clients that they had great faith in their "normal" human constructive processes, and strongly believed in the clients' assets and potentialities. This method of "normalizing" your own thoughts, feelings, and actions has its distinct advantages. You do have many constructive tendencies and can use them to pull yourself out of practical and emotional holes.

When you focus on your assets and your possibilities for change, you can often figure out specific things to do to help yourself — concrete ways of thinking and acting less defeatingly than you now act. If you have the ability to recover easily from business failures, for example, you can see that you also can recover from personal rejection.

For these and other good reasons, by all means see yourself as a "normal" individual, who has some destructive behaviors but who can lead a happy existence in spite of them. As noted in Chapter 8, don't be Pollyannaish in this respect. Don't claim to have special talents that you really don't have, or to be able to marvelously conquer all Adversity. Your failings are handicaps that you'd better acknowledge and work to overcome. But, again, you are not a Failure but a person who is now failing and who can usually correct yourself and do better tomorrow. See yourself in a well-rounded way. Don't overemphasize your deficiencies. Take correcting your ways as a fascinating challenge.

Here are some disadvantages of Pollyannaism:

- You may be temporarily helped by overemphasizing your positive and "normal" traits but you will help yourself to *feel* better and not to *get* better. Getting better consists of fully acknowledging your self-defeating ways and working hard to improve them. Feeling better can interfere with this by helping you deny real failings.

- You may view some of your acts as "normal" or "good" when they are really destructive. Thus, you may think that you are avoiding "dangers" when you are actually exaggerating them. For example, you may view driving as "very dangerous" when you are really making up excuses for not going to the trouble of getting a license and taking care of a car. Your reasons for avoidance are then rationalizations that may unduly restrict you from traveling.

Check out your "normal" behaviors with some close friends or relatives. See if you are healthily acknowledging that you are not "abnormal," or perhaps making up excuses for not working to overcome some of your real problems.

Using — and Misusing — Distraction Methods

As many people have discovered over the centuries, the human mind is often only able to focus adequately on one thing at a time. When, for example, you strongly worry about almost anything, you distract yourself from other things, and often function poorly at school, at work, and at social relations. But when you force yourself, in spite of your worrying, to strongly focus on studying, on work, or how to conduct your social relationships, you usually interrupt your worrying and function rather well. I found this out for myself when, at the age of 19, I was scared witless of public speaking. In the course of presenting a debate I was very anxious about, I prepared a carefully written brief and then strongly focused on its contents while I was speaking. I got so carried away with presenting my subject that I momentarily sidetracked my anxiety and spoke very well.

Ancient thinkers realized that various forms of concentration interfere with anxiety and depression. So they recommended Yoga, breathing exercises, meditation, and other forms of distraction. They also included, as in Zen Buddhism, various rituals and practices which may be useful in their own right but that also serve as distractions and help people to *interrupt* their worrying.

You may therefore use these and other distraction methods when you are anxious, panicked, depressed, enraged, and self-pitying. Edmund Jacobson's progressive relaxation technique, with its gradual focus on relaxing all the major muscles of your body, serves very well in this respect. But so may television, movies, reading, playing games, and many other kinds of entertainment and involvement.

Herbert Benson, who has studied and written about the relaxation response, points out that meditation and other forms of "religious" or "mystical" practice can be done without adding to them any creed or sacred outlook. One form of relaxation exercise that he recommends is this procedure:

Select a word, such as "one," "peace," "om," or a short phrase that has meaning for you. Sit or lie in a comfortable position. Close your eyes and let the muscles of your body relax. Breathe slowly and naturally. As you exhale, keep repeating your word or phrase. Try to disregard other thoughts, but don't try desperately. Remain relaxed and passive if they intrude and go back to focusing on your breathing and repeating your word or phrase. You can use this technique for 5, 10, or 20 minutes whenever you feel overly stressed and anxious. You can also use it for restful practice 10 or 20 minutes every day.

Many other therapists have also recommended various distraction techniques, including Robert Fried, Daniel Goleman, Maurits Kwee, D. H. Shapiro, and R. N. Walsh. Just about all these methods can work if you push yourself to use them. Some of the advantages of using them include the following:

- You can learn many of them quickly and without much effort, especially some of the muscle relaxing, breathing, and meditation techniques.
- When you use them, you can often calm yourself down immediately, within a few minutes. Even when you are in a severe state of panic, if you breathe deeply and/or force yourself to think of pleasant scenes, you may be able to make yourself unpanicked almost immediately.
- Once you use distraction techniques, you may be in a much better frame of mind to use various other methods that I describe in this book. When you remain very upset, you are often less capable of using these methods.
- Some relaxing methods, such as the use of reading, TV, and other forms of entertainment, are enjoyable in their own right and add to your life.
- When you use distraction methods successfully, you see that you really are in control of some of your

thoughts and feelings and get a sense of self-efficacy or achievement-confidence. Very helpful!

- Some distraction techniques may lead to philosophic changes. If you meditate by watching your anxious thoughts, you may conclude that the "terrible" things you are predicting will not actually happen and that even if some of them do occur, you can cope with them and handle them. Seeing your awfulizing from a distance may help you to stop it.

For reasons such as these, many different kinds of distraction may serve you well. However, like many self-therapy methods, they may also have their distinct limitations and may take you away from making the kind of profound philosophical changes that I favor in this book. For example:

- You may distract yourself from your musturbatory and awfulizing ideas, but by no means necessarily change them. You may still remain convinced that you absolutely *must* win someone's approval and that you are a worthless individual if you don't. By meditation, breathing, Yoga, or other focusing methods, you may drive this thought out of your head — temporarily! But soon after you stop using these methods, the thought may easily return. So distracting yourself may help you *feel* better; but it may not help Dispute your crazy notions and thereby *get* better. You may sometimes even use it as an excuse *not* to do the vigorous Disputing that will truly change your Irrational Beliefs: "I already feel better, so why bother to Dispute my unrealistic ideas?"
- Distraction methods may work so well that they stop you from seeing that it is mainly your own self-defeating philosophy that upsets you. They may let you believe that your destructive thoughts just naturally assail you, instead of seeing that you actively bring them on and can therefore effectively change them.
- Because distraction is often easy, while seeing and Disputing your dysfunctional Beliefs is harder, you may indulge in these methods and thereby increase your low frustration tolerance. You may convince yourself that more effective methods of self-therapy are "too hard" and that therefore you "can't" do them or that they are "not worth" doing.

Jody found that her best method of relaxing was to sit in a comfortable chair and picture herself in the midst of a field of daisies, plucking the flowers and greatly enjoying their scent. Whenever she was anxious about her high school teaching job, she could resort to this method and immediately become calm and serene. She even managed, at times, to give her students some work to do so that she could relax at her desk while they were working. She swiftly eased her anxiety about not teaching well and about being taken to task by her principal. She used this relaxing technique whenever she felt her anxiety coming on.

Unfortunately, Jody's anxiety soon returned, and sometimes she used her relaxing method several times a day, as well as at night, when her anxious feelings kept her from sleeping. But her philosophy that she *had to be* the best high school teacher never changed, and she devoted more time to using distraction. When she remained anxious, she resorted to Xanax and other tranquilizers, but found the same thing happening. They quickly made her feel less anxious, but only for a short while. Her doses of sedatives also increased.

Finally, Jody came to one of my workshops on "Overcoming Anxiety" at the Albert Ellis Institute in New York City, started reading REBT books (see References), and got in touch with her perfectionistic demands about teaching. By actively Disputing them and doing some shame-attacking exercises (which I shall describe later), she finally changed her anxiety-creating philosophy and thereafter only occasionally used her distraction technique. She enjoyed her teaching much more and was rarely anxious in class.

By all means, then, learn one or more suitable distraction techniques and use it from time to time when you are agitated and therefore not functioning well. But realize that, for the most part, such techniques *soothe rather than heal* and that they tend to gloss over rather than change your disturbance-creating attitudes. So use them in addition to, rather than instead of, active, vigorous Disputing of your Irrational Beliefs.

Using Spiritual and Religious Methods to Help You With Your Emotional Problems

Various religious and spiritual forms of self-therapy have been used since time immemorial and have had distinct value. Why are they useful? Largely because religious and spiritual views include ideas, meanings, and values. If, therefore, you have a clear-cut destructive philosophy, you may be able to replace it with a religious philosophy that will, first, distract you from your present ideas and, second, help you replace them with a more useful set of ideas.

Some of the notions that are included in various religions that may prove helpful when you are disturbing yourself include these:

- Religious and spiritual ideas and practices are often highly involving and may encourage you to devote yourself to a group, a church, or a cause, that distract you from your disturbed thoughts, feelings, and actions. When you pray, for example, you are occupied with your prayers and not with how "awful" your life is. Studying religious or spiritual texts can also be anxiety-diverting (as various kinds of nonreligious studying can be). Engaging in religious activities with other people can again be very distracting. If you are preoccupied with anxiety, depression, or rage, religious practices can take your focus away from these disturbances and thereby help make you calmer.

- Humans, as Viktor Frankl and other existentialist thinkers have pointed out, seem to be naturally prone to create a central meaning in their lives. If you merely live from moment to moment you may get by reasonably well. But if you have some central goal, purpose, or ideal, you usually feel more involved and happier. There are a good many political, social, economic, family and other meanings that you can acquire, and religion is one of them. In particular, many religions urge their followers to believe in and get devoted to some causes, and to actively work for promoting them with other religionists.

- If you deeply involve yourself in a project or cause, you tend to acquire what Robert Harper and I, in *A Guide to Rational Living*, call a *vital absorbing interest* — that is, one that can occupy you intensely for many years, even for a whole lifetime. If you are truly involved with it and keep working for a cause, the important meaning that it gives you is usually extremely satisfying and provides answers to important questions which you believe in and are enthusiastic about. A vital absorbing interest can also be social — such as working to save our forests — and may aid what Alfred Adler called *healthy social interest*.

- As I have noted before, when you are emotionally disturbed you have harmful negative thoughts and you often have strong faith in these thoughts. Thus, you may believe devoutly that you can't change your ways and that you must continue to be miserable. Most religious and spiritual views give you a set of optimistic instead of pessimistic thoughts. These include the belief that you will benefit from being religious, that God will indubitably help you, that devotion to your religion will greatly benefit others, etc.

These optimistic thoughts may give you faith in yourself and your ability to change. This kind of faith will often help you — just as faith in a particular form of therapy and in your personal therapist may help.

Oddly enough, again, the *object* of your faith may not matter. Thus, you may benefit yourself by devoutly believing in God, in a fairy godmother, in a shaman, or even in the Devil, and you can make yourself absolutely sure that this entity may help you with a headache, with your anxiety, or with your practical problems. When you have this kind of faith, you may benefit in several ways:

- First, from stopping your moaning about your problem — which in itself may tend to help you improve it.
- Second, you may distract yourself from your pain and trouble, and therefore suffer less from it.
- Third, you may calm down and be able to think of measures that may be helpful.
- Fourth, you may give your body a chance to use its natural resources to cope with your physical ailments.
- Fifth, you may tend to "get out of yourself," as AA encourages, and become less self-absorbed.

So, as I note in the revised edition of *Reason and Emotion in Psychotherapy*, even though it is unlikely that your chosen Higher Power will actually do very much to help you, your strong belief that it will may often lead you to feel better and therefore it will be effective.

Any religious or spiritual creed may work for you, as long as you fervently believe in it. The problem is that no religious dogmas are scientifically confirmable nor disconfirmable and that it is only your strong belief in them that really seems to work to make you feel better.

Are you therefore better off refusing to believe that any supernatural beings will help you with your problems? Often, yes; but not necessarily so. I and several other religious followers of REBT — especially the psychologists Brad Johnson and Stevan Nielsen — have shown how absolutistic beliefs are often dangerous to mental health, but some Christian, Jewish, and other religious traditions have developed sensible and workable philosophies that are very similar to helpful REBT views. Thus, the Judeo-Christian Belief that God accepts the sinner but not the sin is similar to the REBT philosophy of Unconditional Self-Acceptance (USA). People who think that they need the backing of a Higher Power to help them think rationally may benefit by holding that Belief, as long as they don't hold it self-defeatingly. Dogmatic religion, then can work for you. However, it also may have disadvantages, such as these:

- Because your believing in anything supernatural cannot really be proven or disproven, and is therefore nonscientific, you can easily become disillusioned about such a belief and make yourself anxious and depressed when it doesn't seem to hold up. This is especially true if you have a Pollyannaish element in your faith. If you hold, for example, that if you pray to God for help, He or She will indubitably help you, watch it!. You may be unrealistically convinced that there is some transformational energy in the Universe that you can tap into to make you give up your addiction to drinking or smoking. Or that your chosen deity or guru will relieve you of any work you have to do to make your life better. These views, of course, can easily prove to be false, and lead to becoming disillusioned.

- When you believe that you *absolutely need* a Higher Power to help you overcome your addiction or other emotional problems, you also tend to think that you cannot do this on your own, without the help of such a power. This, of course, is untrue: millions of individuals who do not believe in any god, guru, or Higher Power obviously help themselves to reduce their disturbances. A good many people are temporarily helped by their belief in such a Power, but then they give up this Belief, and sometimes help themselves more than ever with more realistic Beliefs.

- Belief in any kind of spirit, god, religion or transcendental power, may easily become an addiction in its own right. A high percentage of true believers, as Eric Hoffer showed a number of years ago, are obsessive-compulsive about their religious and spiritual views. Another number of devout believers — similar to the devout followers of fascism, Naziism, Communism, and other creeds which are sometimes atheistic — make themselves so fanatical that they violently oppose members of other groups and nonbelievers, and have often jailed, tortured, and murdered them. This kind of intolerant, obsessive-compulsive behavior can be a disturbance itself and can lead to injustice and social harm.
- Belief in supernatural or transcendental processes may, at times, definitely be helpful but leave you far from the deeper, more intensive, enduring solutions to emotional problems that this book describes. For when you achieve such an elegant solution, you do so through your own thoughts, feelings, and behaviors, and not through outside forces. You therefore almost always have control over your own emotional destiny. You can react to Adversities or obnoxious Activating Events in almost any manner you *choose* to; and you can make yourself healthfully sorry, regretful, and frustrated but not seriously upset about them.

For reasons such as these, relying on religious and spiritual help has its distinct limitations. It may well work for you at times, and if that is the only path you will take, then by all means take it. But there are other, more elegant routes to emotional health and self-fulfillment that you can take. Consider them!

At the same time, if you want to keep your religious beliefs, you can find effective rational philosophies in them. As pointed out by Stevan Nielsen and Brad Johnson — Rational Emotive Behavior Therapy practitioners who believe in God — religious philosophies also include self-helping beliefs of forgiving yourself and others, accepting that which you cannot change while working to solve that which you can change, learning to live with others in an orderly manner, and accepting that you have some degree of free will in decision making.

Gaining Insight Into Your Disturbances and Inadequacies

In spite of its shortcomings in truly helping people with their emotional problems, psychoanalysis is still popular. It probably gets people to spend more time and money for poor results than does any other method so far created. Why? Because people *like* getting insight or understanding into the so-called causes of their disturbances and they *enjoy* endlessly talking about themselves. They also *love* blaming their public speaking phobias on "recovered memories" of early sex abuse!

Does psychoanalytic insight really explain how you got the way you are — how you developed your main disturbances? After being trained in it and using it for six years early in my career, I would say, "Practically never." It sometimes gives you deep "explanations" of how you were influenced by your parents and other significant people during your early years and how these attachments still seriously affect you today. Much of this is interesting and some of it true — because you were very suggestible as a child, did pick up many standards and values, and still retain a number of them at present. So you were (and still are) influenceable. Yes.

But standards, goals, and values do *not*, in themselves, make you disturbed — even when you significantly fail to fulfill them. As I keep repeating, your *musts* and *demands* about these standards are the main culprits. No matter how much you *like* your parents' love, social approval, and cornbread, you don't have to insist that you absolutely *must* have them, and that it is *terrible* when you don't. You were mainly taught that these goals are highly desirable, but not exactly taught that you *absolutely must* have them or else your world will come to an end. You were only partly taught this *must*.

You have some *choice* in what you learn, follow, and retain. You can — as many do — ignore the "right" standards you learn. You can — as many more do — accept these values, believe in them, usually follow them — and still not make them into dire necessities. You also can take your own personal strong desires — for a certain food or the love of a particular person — and make them into "dire needs," even though your family and your culture do not encourage you to demand the fulfillment of these personal goals.

All of this shows that understanding your wishes, wants, standards, and values is interesting and in some ways important in relation to your emotional problems. But often not very much! More important, from an REBT standpoint, your understanding of your *musts* and *demands* plays a vital role in your upsetness and how you can change. And that's exactly what you've been learning in this book. REBT shows you what your specific demands are; how unrealistic, illogical, and impractical they seem to be; and how you can replace them with realistic, logical, and practical preferences.

Where and how you got your musts is also interesting, but usually not too important. You probably took many of your desires from your upbringing — you *agreed* when your parents and teachers told you that *you'd better* perform well and earn social approval. But then you imposed your own interpretation, went beyond parental expectations and decided you *absolutely had to* do well. Or you developed some of your own strong desires and easily — partly because of your innate grandiosity — *made* them into arrogant commands to yourself.

Does it matter exactly *how* you actually came to musturbate? Probably not, unless you are writing your autobiography. Go review your history, if you wish, and find out — if you ever can. If you can't, no great loss. As long as you discover what your main musts are, how they encourage you to make yourself disturbed, and what you can do to change them, enough already!

Back to the present! Whatever the "original source" of your disturbance, you are *now* in its throes. What are you *now* going to do to alleviate it? Return to REBT's Insights No. 1, No. 2, and No. 3! Understand them — and use them. Here they are again for a quick review:

(1) "I don't just *get* upset but mainly *upset myself.*"
(2) "No matter when and how I *started* disturbing myself about Adversities, I am *still* doing so today."
(3) "*Insight* isn't enough. Only much *work and practice* will help me change my self-defeating thoughts, feelings, and actions."

Enhancing Your Self-Efficacy and Self-Esteem

Two methods that are widely used by therapists but that have their limitations and hazards are *increasing your sense of self-effi-cacy* and *enhancing your self-esteem*. Self-efficacy is a term popu-larized and well-researched by Albert Bandura and his students. It is a synonym for what I called *achievement-confidence* in 1962, and means that you see that you can perform some task well — such as playing the piano or doing math — and you, therefore, have a high degree of confidence that you can competently repeat it. As many experiments have shown, if you have self-efficacy, you can usually perform better at certain life activities than if you have a sense of self-inefficacy. So that is quite helpful!

However, you can acquire a *false* sense of self-efficacy when you *think* you do well at something but you actually do poorly. Oddly enough, while your false confidence may actually help you do better at this task, it may also lead to disillusionment, less confidence, and self-downing. So the way to get to a good sense of self-efficacy is to practice, practice, practice. Then you can do well — and know that you can.

Self-efficacy frequently leads to a feeling of self-esteem — which is dangerous and often poisonous to your mental health. How so? Because when you have high self-esteem you rate your *self* and your *essence*, along with your *performances*. You commonly tell yourself, "Because I do this important thing — math, sports, socializing, loving, or almost anything else — I am therefore *a good, competent person!*" Great ego feeling!

Unfortunately, self-esteem includes its opposite: *self-disesteem* or *self-hatred*. "Because I do this important thing *badly*, I am therefore a *bad, incompetent person!*" Where will that idea get you? Depressed and anxious. Depressed when you perform poorly; anxious when you are afraid that you *may* screw up. Because you are always a fallible, imperfect individual, you can easily make yourself, with *this* philosophy, perennially anxious and depressed.

Self-esteem is a good feeling that is very fragile. Its flipside is self-downing. It tends to create so much anxiety and depression that it often sabotages your self-efficacy. So at times applaud your deeds and actions, but not your *self* or *essence*. Go, instead, for the kind of unconditional self-acceptance (USA) that I keep advocating in this book. That is a much deeper and more elegant solution.

11

Feeling Ways to Make Yourself Less Disturbable

When I was a teenager, the novels of H. G. Wells, Tolstoy, Turgeniev, Dostoevsky, Sinclair Lewis, Upton Sinclair, Theodore Dreiser, and others and the dramas of Ibsen, Shaw, Chekhov, Strindberg, O'Neill, and other serious playwrights led me into philosophy. I soon began to use philosophical ideas on myself to overcome my native tendencies to be anxious and insecure.

I originally allowed myself to be guided by a number of ancient and modern philosophers, as well as by a few psychologists, who pointed out that if you want to change your feelings and behaviors, the quickest and best way is to change your thinking. For some of us this is sometimes true. Including me. When I first used ancient and modern philosophy to mend my own emotional ways, however, I was so intrigued by doing so, and I so much enjoyed my trying to change my self-defeating ideas into more effective ones, that I found the work of doing so amazingly easy. Maybe problem solving is just my thing. Easy!

Not so with the great majority of my clients. When I started doing therapy in 1943 (before I sidetracked myself by doing psychoanalysis in 1947), I was quite active-directive and had no hesitation in applying some of the sensible ideas I had learned from reading and from using philosophy to conquer my own anxiety.

What a job! I soon found, as I started doing Rational Emotive Behavior Therapy in 1955, that most of my clients agreed that they had Irrational Beliefs (IB's), and that they'd better change them for more rational Beliefs (RB's). Nonetheless they often vigorously and forcefully held on to their IB's. Even when they said, "Yes, I guess I *don't* have to always succeed at important projects," they lightly held this RB, and they simultaneously strongly believed, "But I really *do*!" Being members of the human (all too human!) race, they easily held two contradictory Beliefs at the same time. They *really* believed the irrational one more strongly, and they largely acted upon that one.

Well! What could I do about that to help my still disturbed clients? Fairly obviously: Somehow induce them to *strongly* Dispute their IB's and to *powerfully* affirm their RB's until they truly weakened the former and strengthened the latter. Simple — but not easy!

I also realized that weak preferences ("I dislike your lying to me.") usually lead to weak emotions (such as mild hostility) while strong demands ("I hate your lying to me, so you *must* not lie!") tend to lead to self-defeating emotions such as intense rage. So I created and adapted a number of forceful emotive methods — *hot* cognitions and feelings — that now are often used by REBT practitioners.

You can use these methods to weaken your Irrational Beliefs and strengthen your rational ones. In this chapter I've presented some of the best of them.

Using Strong Coping Self-Statements

You can create the same kind of coping self-statements that I described in Chapter 9 and say them to yourself very powerfully until you really convince yourself of — and truly *feel* — their messages. For example:

Strong Realistic Self-statements: "I *never, never need* what I want, no matter how much I *prefer* it!" "I CAN give up my addiction if I keep forcing myself to go through the pain of withdrawal!"

Strong Logical Self-statements: "Even though I failed in several relationships, this doesn't mean that I *have* to fail again. No, I don't *have to*! I CAN have a successful relationship!" "If I work hard at this job I'll *probably* win my boss's approval, but it doesn't follow that he therefore *must* approve of me and give me a raise! No connection!"

Strong Practical Self-statements: "Demanding that my friend *absolutely must* lend me money will only make me anxious and angry. Yes, *really* anxious. And *very* angry! I'd better *wish* for a loan but not *demand* it." "If I convince myself that I *absolutely need* to have good weather so that I can play tennis tomorrow where will that get me? Nowhere! Only extremely anxious and depressed — and my anxiety and depression will not affect the weather at all!"

If you resoundingly repeat these coping self-statements, either aloud or in your head, and if you strongly think about them and prove how correct they are, you will more likely believe and act on them than if you repeat them weakly. Note how REBT coping statements use the same Effective New Philosophies (E's) derived as answers to your Disputing (D) your Irrational Beliefs (IB's). Therefore, they are more accurate than unrealistic kinds of positive thinking.

Using Rational Emotive Imagery

REBT uses several imagery methods because imagination is a powerful thinking and emotional process. Maxie Maultsby, Jr., a rational behavior psychiatrist who studied with me in the 1960s, created Rational Emotive Imagery (REI) in 1971. Finding REI an effective cognitive-emotive method, I modified it, made it even more emotive, and have successfully used it for a quarter of a century with thousands of clients and with hundreds of volunteers at my workshops.

Let me illustrate how I used Rational Emotive Imagery with Marty, a 35-year-old mechanic, who was thoroughly ashamed of his overeating and of being fifty pounds overweight. In our first few sessions, we discovered that he strongly believed, when he kept stuffing cake and candy bars in his mouth, "I *must not* be deprived of this delicious stuff! I *can't stand* such horrible frustration! Life is hardly worth living when I'm racked with hunger!"

Once he stuffed himself and realized that he was going to gain even more weight, Marty beat himself in this fashion: "Look what I've done! Pigged out again! I *should* know better but I don't! What an idiot I am! I hate myself."

Marty and I agreed that he had these Beliefs, that they were irrational, and that he could and preferably should give them up. But he didn't. He only lightly believed, "I don't *have to* eat, even when I'm hungry; and it's really stupid of me to pig out but that doesn't make me a stupid, rotten person!" So he continued to overeat and to defame himself.

I used Rational Emotive Imagery with Marty in this fashion: "Close your eyes and imagine one of the worst possibilities: You keep eating cake and candy bars incessantly and keep gaining more pounds every week. You promise yourself to stop but you don't. If anything, you eat more than usual during and between meals. Your friends and family are revolted by your foolish behavior. Can you vividly imagine that?"

"Oh, yes. Easily."

"How do you feel — really feel — in your gut, as you visualize yourself gulping down the extra, unnecessary food?"

"Awful! Like a total slob. A weak — really weak — crumb. Very depressed."

"Good. I think you are honestly in touch with your feelings. So really keep feeling them. Feel low, down, depressed, like a total slob. Feel it. Focus on your rotten feelings."

"Oh, I really do. Very depressed. Very much of a no-good worm!"

"Fine! Feel deeply, feel deeply. And now that you feel so low, so depressed, keep the same image of you foolishly stuffing yourself — don't change the image. But while you picture it, work on your feelings — which you are able to do — and change them to healthy negative feelings. Keep the same image but make yourself feel only *sorry* and *disappointed* about your self-defeating behavior. Only *sorry* and *disappointed*, not depressed, not like a real worm."

"Can I actually do that?" Marty asked.

"Of course you can," I replied. It's *your* feeling and *you* created it. So you always have the ability to change it. Try! See!"

After two minutes of silence, in the course of which he was obviously struggling with himself, Marty said, "O.K., I did it."

"And you now feel?"

"Sorry, very sorry. And quite disappointed with what I was doing, how I was stuffing myself."

"Any feeling of depression?"

"No, not really. Sadness but not depression."

"Good! Very good! What did you do to change your feelings?"

"I talked to myself, as we had discussed before. But this time I talked more vigorously, since I had to fight against my depressed feelings. So I said to myself, 'Too bad you slipped again, Buster. Really idiotic! But you're not *a complete idiot*. Just a fallible person who still at times acts very stupidly. Too bad! — but you're still okay.'"

"Fine. That was really good. That will work to make you feel sorry and disappointed rather than depressed. Now you can *keep* feeling healthily sorry and disappointed by doing this same exercise once a day for the next 30 days, until you begin to automatically feel disappointed with your behavior and not damning *you* for it. It will only take you a couple of minutes a day to do it, and you will soon see what good results you will get."

"Once a day?"

"Yes, every day. Once a day, until whenever you imagine yourself foolishly overeating, or even when you actually do pig out, you will have trained yourself to feel automatically *sorry* and *disappointed* — and *not* like a *lowly slob or a worm.*"

"That would be good."

"Yes, it would be. Now will you contract with yourself to do this Rational Emotive Imagery once a day until you feel healthily sorry instead of unhealthily depressed?"

"Yes, I agree to do it. And if I don't follow through — what?"

"You can use reinforcement or operant conditioning to help you follow through. Let me show you. What do you really like to do, that you tend to do practically every day of the week, just because you like it?"

"Let me see," Marty said. "Well — playing ping pong. I really enjoy that."

"Good. For the next 30 days only allow yourself to play ping pong *after* you've done the Rational Emotive Imagery and changed your feelings. Then you can play all the ping pong you want."

"And if I want to play early in the day?"

"Do the REI before you play. It only takes a couple of minutes."

"But suppose I *still* avoid doing REI?"

"Then you can also set yourself a penalty or a punishment."

"Like what?"

"Well, what do you hate to do, and therefore try to avoid doing? Some task or chore you really detest and that would be a punishment?"

"How about cleaning the bathroom. I hate that."

"Fine. If your bedtime arrives on any day for the next month, and you still haven't done Rational Emotive Imagery and changed your feelings that day, make yourself clean your bathroom for an hour. If you've done it, no bathroom cleaning that day. O.K.?"

"O.K. I'm sure that will help me do the Rational Emotive Imagery."

"I'm sure it will!"

Marty did carry through and only occasionally had to use a reinforcement or punishment to help him do so. After using REI for 22 days in a row he did start to automatically feel sorry and disappointed when he vividly imagined himself overeating. On the one day that he actually did pig out on cake and candy, he also felt sorry and disappointed, but did not put himself down, and went right back to his diet of no extra cake and candy.

So try REI yourself, especially if you have trouble believing your own rational coping statements. Work on changing your unhealthy negative feelings to more healthy ones. You largely feel the way you think. So change some of your self-statements to minimize your anxiety, depression, and rage. Think better and feel better. You *can* control your emotional destiny.

Use Shame-Attacking Exercises

I realized, soon after I started doing psychotherapy in the early 1940s, that shame is the essence of much — no, not all! — human disturbance. When you feel ashamed, embarrassed, or humiliated about something you have done — or have not done — you are observing that, first, you did the wrong thing — something that other people would criticize. But even then you could tell yourself, "I'm sorry that I acted badly and that people are criticizing me for that. But I don't have to take my wrong act or their criticism too seriously. I'll try to do better next time." If you think this way, you will *not* feel ashamed but only *sorry* and *regretful*. Then you are thinking and feeling healthily and have no severe emotional problem.

To feel deep shame, however, you're also telling yourself something like this: "I *absolutely should not* have done what I did! How *terrible!* I am a *rotten person* for doing it and deserve to be put down by others!" To make yourself *only* feel sorry and disappointed about your "shameful" behavior, you can give up your musturbation and return to *wishing* — but not *demanding* — that you act better. Yes, wishing.

Because, however, you may have a strong tendency to keep making yourself unhealthily ashamed when you do something "wrong" and blameworthy, I invented a shame-attacking exercise in 1968 to give you emotive and behavioral practice in overcoming intense feelings of shame. Thus exercise is one of the main emotive methods of helping you to achieve unconditional self-acceptance (USA).

Here is how I explain the now-famous shame-attacking exercise to my lecture and workshop audiences, after first introducing it with the gist of the last three paragraphs above:

"Think of something you might do that you personally consider shameful, foolish, ridiculous, embarrassing, or humiliating. Not something you might do for fun but something you would really feel quite ashamed of doing. Not something, of course, that would harm anyone — such as slapping someone in the face. Not something that might harm you — such as telling your boss or supervisor that he or she is no good. Not something that might land you in jail — such as insulting a cop. This should be something that you would consider shameful, that other people might put you down for, but that would not get you or anyone else in real trouble.

"Now this exercise has two important parts. First, *do* this shame-attacking exercise frequently — *in public*. Second, work on your feelings — as you do it and afterward — to *not* feel ashamed. Feel *sorry* and *disappointed* with your 'shameful' behavior, perhaps, but *not ashamed*, not self-downing, not like a lowly person.

"What can you do? Again, anything that you would ordinarily feel ashamed of doing. Some of the most popular ones that our clients at the Institute for Rational Emotive Therapy keep doing are yelling out the stops in a subway or other train, telling a stranger that 'I just got out of the mental hospital and would like to know what month it is,' and walking a banana on a leash and feeding it with another banana.

Okay. Think it over. Try one of these shame-attacking exercises — or any one that you would feel ashamed to do. Do one or more of these exercises, work on *not* feeling ashamed or embarrassed, and you may help yourself considerably!"

As I noted above, tens of thousands of REBT clients and readers have used shame-attacking exercises to help themselves reduce their self-downing. Try them and see!

Using REBT Role-Playing

REBT has borrowed the technique of role-playing that was origi-nated by J. L. Moreno and popularized by Raymond Corsini and others. But in REBT we have added some unusual aspects to it.

You can first use it behaviorally, by having a friend or relative role-play an interviewer, supervisor, boss, teacher, or anyone else you have trouble performing with or are anxious about. Your partner can deliberately give you a hard time during the interview and you can do your best to respond to her or him adequately. Stop the role play after you have talked for awhile, and ask your partner and preferably other observers to criticize your performance. Discuss and model how to improve it, and keep practicing until you get still better. This is a form of behavior rehearsal and often works very well.

The REBT "extra" in this role-playing is to watch for your becoming anxious, depressed, or angry in the course of your performance, to temporarily stop the role-playing, and for you, your partners, and your onlookers to discover exactly what you are thinking to *make yourself* upset. Find and Dispute your Irrational Beliefs leading to your upsetness, and work at changing these Beliefs to Effective New Philosophies that will minimize it. Using this aspect of REBT, your role-playing takes on an additional *emotive* aspect and is more experiential than is regular Disputing. This form of role-playing helps immediately to bring out some of the disturbed feelings that you may otherwise not risk experiencing. It also helps you deal with these feelings while they are actually arising, and not merely in between sessions or after you have experienced them in the past.

Reverse Role-Playing

If you have trouble changing your unhealthy, Irrational Beliefs to healthier Rational Beliefs, you may want to try reverse role-playing with one of your friends or associates. To do this, tell your partner one of your Irrational Beliefs (IB's) — such as, "I *absolutely need* John (or Joan) to love me, and I can't enjoy life *at all* without his (or her) undivided affection!"

Your role-playing partner then adopts your IB and holds on to it, powerfully and rigidly, while you try to get the partner to give it up. No go! Your partner won't relent, and gives you great practice in actively and vigorously Disputing your own dysfunctional Belief. As you practice Disputing very forcefully and persistently, you really see how crazy some of your ideas are, observe how you strongly and ridiculously cling to them, and learn how you can finally let go of them. Once again, as in behavior rehearsal, your role-playing partner(s), and perhaps some onlookers (if you're working in a group situation), critique your ways of Disputing your partner's IB's (which are really your own), and suggest more effective kinds of Disputation that you can use.

Using Humor to Refuse to Take Things Too Seriously

To take things seriously, and especially to create a serious vital absorbing interest in a subject/hobby/activity, will probably help you enjoy life considerably. Not so, however, if you take things *too* seriously! Disturbance largely consists of giving things importance and then greatly *exaggerating* that importance, slipping in the *have to* and the *got to*. For instance, if you say, "I very much *want* to do well at science or at art," you will push yourself to do well, will be nicely occupied while doing so, and probably will help yourself succeed. But if you jump to, "I *absolutely must* do well at science or art!" you will make yourself anxious about not succeeding and will probably do relatively poorly. Even when you are doing well, you will worry about doing worse in the future; and you may not enjoy your achievements.

Humor can help your overly-serious musturbation. It reduces the sacredness of your thoughts, shows you that you can laugh at your failures, and indicates that succeeding and being approved by others is still important — but not all-important. Instead of your seeing the end of the world when you fail or get rejected, humor shows you that it doesn't end — and that other interesting possibilities may follow. If anything punctures your grandiosity, and brings you back to being a fallible but acceptable human, humor does this trick. Humor laughs at your flaws — but in *an accepting and tolerant way.*

So look at the flip side of the foolish things that you think or do. See the irony of trying too hard and not being able to enjoy the process of trying. See the stupidity of taking things *too* seriously — whether it be your own mistakes, the failings of others, the shabby ways in which you are treated, and even the needless pains that you foolishly bring on yourself.

Particularly laugh at your perfectionism. As a human, you're just not going to be perfect — well, maybe occasionally at a few specific tasks. But to strive desperately for constant perfection is to take things too seriously — and that is laughable.

Consider how ironic it is to believe that you can change *others* — which you usually *can't* — and at the same time to insist that you can't change *yourself* — which is the one thing that (if you work hard at it) you usually *can* do!

I have been a songwriter since I was 15, when I saw that the lyrics to most popular songs are downright silly, not to mention highly Pollyannaish. Your passionate love for Ms. X or Mr. Y is not going to last forever; and they certainly won't madly love you for an eternity. When your beloved leaves you (or unfortunately dies), you may remember or love him or her for the rest of your days, but you'd better not foolishly kill yourself, as innumerable ballads tell you that you should naturally want to do. Love and sex may truly be your greatest thing in the world, at least for awhile. But they really don't make the world go round. There truly are other fine things in life — many good reasons to go on living and contributing to the well-being of yourself and others.

From 1943 onward I had found that making fun of some of my clients' Irrational Beliefs — though not of the *people* who held these Beliefs — often helped them. Especially in my several REBT group therapy sessions every week, I found that joking about some of my clients' problems and taking them to humorous extremes lightened up our sessions and helped them to see how they exaggerated the significance of many things.

At the 1976 Annual Convention of the American Psychological Association in Washington, D.C., I gave a talk on humor and psychotherapy. I decided to include some of my rational humorous songs in my presentation and recorded some of them to present. Alas, my tape recorder broke down, so I had to sing them live — in my godawful baritone. To my surprise, they went over wonderfully well — in spite of my singing. So since that time, I have included some of these songs in most of my talks and workshops. At the psychological clinic of the Albert Ellis Institute we give a sheet of them to all our new clients. They then can sing an anti-anxiety song to themselves when they are anxious, an anti-depression song when they are depressed, and so on.

Here are a few of these rational humorous songs that you can use when you are too serious about various things in your life.

WHINE, WHINE, WHINE!
(Tune: Yale Whiffenpool Song, By Guy Scull — A Harvard Man!)
I cannot have all of my wishes filled —
Whine, whine, whine!
I cannot have every frustration stilled —
Whine, whine, whine!
Life really owes me the things that I
*   miss,*
Fate has to grant me eternal bliss!
And since I must settle for less than
*   this —*
Whine, whine, whine!

PERFECT RATIONALITY
(Tune: Funiculi, Funicula, by Luigi Denza)

Some think the world must have a right
*   direction,*
And so do I! And so do I!
Some think that, with the slightest
*   imperfection,*
They can't get by — and so do I!
For I, I have to prove I'm superhuman,
And better far than people are!
To show I have miraculous acumen —
And always rate among the Great!
Perfect, perfect rationality
Is, of course, the only thing for me!
How can I ever think of being
If I must live fallibly?
Rationality must be a perfect thing for
*   me!*

LOVE ME, LOVE ME, ONLY ME!
(Tune: Yankee Doodle Dandy)

Love me, love me, only me
Or I'll die without you!
O, make your love a guarantee,
So I can never doubt you!
Love me, love me totally — really, really
*   try, dear.*

But if you demand love, too
I'll hate you till I die, dear!
Love me, love me all the time,
Thoroughly, and wholly!
Life turns into slushy slime
Unless you love me solely!
Love me with great tenderness,
With no ifs and buts, dear.
If you love me somewhat less,
I'll hate your goddamned guts, dear!

YOU FOR ME AND ME FOR ME
(Tune: Tea for Two, by Vincent Youmans)

Picture you upon my knee,
Just you for me, and me for me!
And then you'll see
How happy I will be!
Though you beseech me,
You never will reach me,
For I am autistic
As any real mystic!
And only relate to
Myself with a great to-do, dear!
If you dare to try to care
You'll see my caring soon will wear,
For I can't pair and make our sharing
*   fair!*
If you want a family,
We'll both agree you'll baby me —
Then you'll see how happy I will be!

I WISH I WERE NOT CRAZY!
(Tune: Dixie, by Dan Emmet)

Oh, I wish I were really put together —
Smooth and fine as patent leather!
Oh, how great to be rated innately
*   sedate!*
But I'm afraid that I was fated
To be rather aberrated —
Oh, how sad to be mad as my Mom and
*   my Dad!*

Oh, I wish I were not crazy! Hooray,
   hooray!
I wish my mind were less inclined
To be the kind that's hazy!
I could, you see, agree to be less crazy
But I, alas, am just too goddamned lazy!

Lyrics by Albert Ellis, Ph.D.
© by the Albert Ellis Institute, 1977-1990.

Reframing the ABC's of Emotional Disturbance

Human perception, thinking, feeling, and behavior all have their limitations and may not always be what they at first seem to be. We are prejudiced by the thoughts and philosophies that we bring to the things that happen to us. We often do not perceive our feelings accurately. We even look at our behaviors in different ways at different times. If you just observe the testimony in any important trial, you will see that the opposing attorneys, the witnesses, and several of the jurors all see things quite differently from each other — and they often make it practically impossible to discover the "true" details of the alleged crime.

When you are emotionally disturbed about something, you had therefore better be skeptical about how you see the ABC's of your disturbance. Take A, for example. A is normally an Activating Event that is against your interests — some kind of Adversity, such as failure, lack of approval, or discomfort. But these Adversities often differ greatly in the eyes of the beholder. If you get an F in a course, you normally would view that as a failure. But you might think that you succeeded because you were able to finish the course, get a few questions on the final exam correct, and learn a good deal in spite of the fact that you failed the course. If you get a B in another course, you may view it as a "horrible failure," because you *should have* got an A or an A+.

Adversities (A's) are particularly hard to evaluate, because of the biased views you bring to them. Suppose you strongly desire to have a child and you and your mate are, so far, infertile and your chances of having a child are slim. You may view this "fact" as absolute — conclude that you never can possibly bear (or have your mate bear) a child. But have you really obtained all the data and *proven* that there is no chance, a little chance, or even a fair chance of pregnancy occurring?

Even if you know for certain that you and your mate are infertile, do you have to view this fact as *a total* loss? Can you view it as a *great,* or even a *moderate* loss? Will you feel good, bad, or indifferent about the possibility of adopting a child? Can you work in a setting — such as a nursery school — where you have steady contact with children? Can you considerably enjoy your friends' or relatives' children?

Obviously, you have *choices* about how you perceive and evaluate the Adversities of your life. So whenever you feel anxious, depressed, or enraged about them, check to see how important their occurrence "really" is. See whether you can *change* these A's, and what good substitutes for them you can get if they are unfulfilling. You can also reframe your *view* of your A's and see that they are not *as* bad as you may have seen them.

Beatrice wanted very much to be a CPA but kept failing the qualifying exam, and concluded that she would never make it. At first, she felt devastated, thought of giving up accounting, and was severely depressed about this possibility. I helped her to check out her Adversity, to see whether it really was impossible for her ever to pass the CPA exam. Apparently, it wasn't, since she was eligible to take the exam again and might pass it.

If she never became a CPA, Beatrice assumed that she couldn't do good work as an accountant. But she was already working well and her present firm was willing to keep her whether or not she ever achieved CPA status.

Beatrice also assumed that if she quit accounting, she could not find another good profession. But we figured out that she could do several related things — such as be an actuary. As a result of our first few sessions, Beatrice began to see the A's of her life quite differently. They were hardly as hopeless as she first viewed them.

We then turned to her Bs, her Belief that she *absolutely must* achieve CPA status. She soon realized that it was not *necessary* that she achieve it. She could still enjoy accounting and make a good living without becoming a CPA.

Beatrice also, with my help, looked at C, her Consequences, her feelings of depression about failing to be a CPA. These were, naturally, bad. But she was also making them much worse, by depressing herself about her depression — convincing herself that she was a worthless person, first, for not being a CPA and, second, for being depressed. When she took another look at her depression, she saw that it indeed was unfortunate, but she didn't have to put herself down for experiencing it. So she worked at having unconditional self-acceptance (USA) while she was still depressed, and she did so well that she gave up her depression about her depression — and also her depression about not yet becoming a CPA!

Beatrice's case shows that you can reframe your perceptions of your Adversities (A's), of your Beliefs about your Adversities (B's), and of your disturbed emotional Consequences (C's). You can, of course, become Pollyannaish, and even make yourself *happy* about the Adversities you encounter. But this has its dangers! Better, you can see these Adversities as challenges to be dealt with, and in that sense can even be partly glad that they are occurring. After failing her CPA exam several times, Beatrice finally saw it as a challenge to find methods of passing it in the future, and as a challenge to not depress herself if she never passed it. She also saw it as an invitation, if she decided to do so, to find some other suitable profession.

You, too, can almost always make your Adversities into challenges to conquer, to remove, to change around, or to live successfully with when you cannot find a practical way out of them. Almost all of them have some good points, if you look for them. Failing to become a CPA, for example, had the advantage of giving Beatrice more time and energy for other pursuits. Failing in a love affair gives you the freedom to get involved in new affairs. Losing a job gives you the opportunity to find a better one — or even to prepare for a more interesting kind of work. Being rejected by a new acquaintance gives you the benefit of staying away from someone who doesn't like you — and getting rid of that person fast!

When people treat you shabbily or unfairly at A (Activating Experience) you can also check their intentions and their motives for doing so. Did they really *intend* to plague you — or were they just thoroughly absorbed in their own interests? Did they actually *see* that they were treating you unjustly — or did they view their acts as fair and just? Were they truly *able* to treat you well — or were they so inept that they could hardly live up to standards of fair treatment? Look at these possibilities, and you may still view their actions as unfortunate and unfair, without inventing evil intentions that they may not have.

Beatrice, for example, thought that it was terribly unfair of her boss not to relieve her of some of her accounting work for a couple of months before her last CPA exam, as she had asked him to do, in order to give herself more time to study. She was very angry at him for his unfairness, until she thought things over and realized that he and his firm had economic difficulties and could not afford to give her the time off that she requested. Realizing this, she lost her anger against him, stopped obsessing about his "horrible" treatment of her, and was able to devote herself better to her studying.

If you go for an elegant — REBT! — solution to your emotional problems, you will see that one of your greatest challenges is to refuse to upset yourself about just about any Adversity that occurs. You may find it relatively easy to refuse to make yourself anxious or depressed when minor misfortunes happen. But when you really work at making yourself less disturbable, you can think in advance about major Adversities — such as the loss of a really fine job or the death of one of your close relatives — and accept the challenge of making yourself *very disappointed and sorry*, but still *not miserably depressed*, about this bad situation. If you really get yourself to believe that nothing in life is *awful*, no matter how sad it is, refusing to upset yourself can be made into one of the key points of your existence. You can make this kind of challenge help you to ward off needless pain and also make working on the challenge enjoyable.

An excellent REBT way of reframing the wrongs and injustices that may happen to you is to look at the Irrational Beliefs (IB's) that others are probably believing when they treat you badly. As noted above, Beatrice reframed her boss's refusal to give her extra time to study for her CPA exam by acknowledging that he and his firm had their own financial problems, and quite possibly could not afford to give her the time she wanted. But she also thought that her boss was somewhat unreasonable about this, because the firm was not exactly going bankrupt, and he could survive if he gave her some time off. So, with my help, she asked herself: "What is he probably telling himself when he refuses my request for extra time off? What are some of his dogmatic *shoulds* and *musts* that are making him act unreasonably?"

She soon came up with an answer: "I think he is telling himself that his firm's schedule of work *absolutely must not* be interrupted and that it would be *awful* if I were not available for a few weeks to handle some of my best accounts. He's insisting that he *couldn't stand* the hassle that would result and that if my clients criticized him for my not being available as usual, that would make him an *inadequate person*, and make him feel very ashamed."

Figuring this out, Beatrice understood better than ever her boss's refusal to give her extra time off for studying; and although she still felt displeased about his having a hang-up, she accepted him with his emotional problems, and again felt much less angry at his refusal.

So whenever you are upset, look at the ABC's of your upsetness, and try to see them in an accurate light. They often have many sides, and your first-blush perceptions may not be accurate — or final. When you see them more clearly you will be less likely to make federal cases of hassles, to horrify yourself about them, and to upset yourself over your upsetness.

If your Adversities (A's) are really difficult — acknowledge that they are indeed a problem. Try to see coping with them as a real challenge. Why not see how adventurous it could be to tackle your problems?

Forceful Disputing of Irrational Beliefs

When you (and other people) dispute your Irrational Beliefs (IB's), you often learn how to do so and come up with useful answers quickly. This is partly because the usual questions you ask yourself when you Dispute are common and obvious, and the answers to them are also — from a realistic, logical, and practical standpoint — fairly clear.

Suppose, for example, that you insist, "I *absolutely must* win the love of Joan (or John), otherwise I am a thoroughly unlovable person who doesn't deserve any good things in life, who will not get any of them, and who might as well become a hermit!" You can discover your IBs and obviously ask yourself, "Where is the evidence that I absolutely must win Joan's (or John's) love? How does it follow that failing to win it makes me a thoroughly unlovable person? Even if I were unlovable, how does it make me undeserving of any of the good things in life? How do I know that I never will get any of these things? What good will becoming a hermit do — how will that make me more lovable, more deserving, or happier? If I strongly hold to these Irrational Beliefs, where will they get me? Will they help me succeed with Joan (or John)? Will they make me less anxious and depressed? Will they help me have a happier life?"

You can answer these questions easily, and thereby "prove" to yourself that: you *don't* absolutely have to win John (or Joan's)

love; that failing to win it will never make you a thoroughly
unlovable person or prevent you from getting any of life's
pleasures; that the universe doesn't include "deservingness"; and
that you will mainly be anxious and depressed if you stick with
these self-defeating, Irrational Beliefs.

Marvelous! But as I have noted often before, *telling* yourself
these Effective New Philosophies hardly amounts to truly
believing them. As a human, you have the ability to tell them to
yourself *weakly* and *lightly* and, simultaneously, to convince
yourself *strongly* and *heavily* of their opposites. You also have
the ability to parrot almost any self-helping statements, and
even to remain unconvinced after you tell them to yourself many
times. Why do you have this ability or disability? Probably
because your strong desires and habits often block your rational
thinking. Thus, when you "know" that you do not have enough
money to purchase something you strongly want, you may still
convince yourself that you do have enough, and may run up a
credit card debt that will get you into serious trouble.

Myron, for example, was told by Massina that she cared very
much for him as a friend but for was not romantically attracted
to him and therefore would not live with him. He told himself
that he'd better stop proposing to her and try going with other
women who cared for him romantically. He kept focusing,
however, on how much Massina enjoyed talking with him and
going to cultural events with him and kept convincing himself
that someday she would really fall in love with him and that they
would have a beautiful marriage. Even when Massina married
someone else, Myron never gave up the idea that she would
eventually divorce her husband and see that he, Myron, was the
right man for her. He finally married Elizabeth, who was very
much enamored of him and proved to be an almost perfect mate,
but he kept hopefully thinking about Massina, which blocked
him from really enjoying his relationship with Elizabeth.

Finally I induced Myron to very powerfully, and quite often,
use this disputation method to prove to himself that Massina
would never love him in the way he wanted and that his
obsession with her would not get him anywhere. He then still
admired and occasionally thought about Massina but he stopped
convincing himself that someday he would walk off into the
sunset with her and he settled down to enjoying his life with
Elizabeth. In fact, he almost beat up on himself for not
managing to do so sooner. But I helped him criticize his
stubbornness without downing *himself* for having it.

Teri was exceptionally angry for several weeks about being crushed against a gum-clacking teenage girl in a crowded subway. She insisted to her therapy group that this girl "s*hould have known* that she was bothering me and other people, and *should have* stopped clacking her gum in this impossibly crowded train." Although Teri knew REBT quite well, and often helped other group members when they were irrationally incensed about someone treating them "unfairly," she at first couldn't give up her obsessive hatred for the girl in the subway. On the spur of the moment, seeing that we were not getting anywhere with her, I got her to agree to take a cassette recorder, state the Irrational Beliefs that were making her furious, and then very powerfully Dispute them until she gave them up.

At first, Teri did some inaccurate Disputing, and stubbornly came up with some wrong ideas: that the offensive girl *absolutely should* not be the way she indubitably was; that she thoroughly deserved to be drawn and quartered — by Teri herself, of course. (Teri would, in the conclusion of this irrational fantasy, be exonerated by twelve respectable jurors and commended by the Judge for completely annihilating this obnoxious girl.) The following week, Teri effectively Disputed her Beliefs that the girl deserved to be severely punished for her crime, but did so in a namby-pamby manner. She was still enraged. At the urging of her therapy group, Teri did her tape-recorded Disputing for the third time, forced herself to do it very vigorously, and got it to sink into her head and her gut. Finally, almost three weeks after this "vile" incident occurred, she was able to accept the girl as a fallible, screwed-up individual who did the wrong thing but who deserved to live and lead a happy existence.

Following this method — which I have used since the 1970s in individual and group therapy with hundreds of disturbed individuals — you can take a cassette recorder, record one of your irrational, self-disturbing beliefs, and then strongly Dispute it a number of times, until you really convince yourself that it is irrational, that it will bring you poor results, and that you can change it to a strong preference instead of a command. Don't stop Disputing your IB until, when you and your friends listen to your recording, they agree that it is sufficiently powerful, and that the Effective New Philosophies that you arrive at are truly sinking into your head and your heart. You may find that, at first, you are not convincing yourself of your realistic and logical conclusions. You may see that you are only lightly believing them. If you persist, you can almost always vigorously believe them, and thereby change your unhealthy feelings and actions into much healthier ones.

Using Paradoxical Interventions

A number of ancient thinkers, including the Zen Buddhists, discovered that humans are often quite paradoxical: They upset themselves even more than usual when they desperately try to unupset themselves. When you feel panicked, if you keep strongly telling yourself, "I *must not* be panicked! It's *awful* to be panicked! I *can't stand* being panicked!" you will often bring on greater and more prolonged feelings of panic. Why? Because these IB's include the implicit notions that panic is *terrible*, that you *cannot* get control of yourself, and that dire things will happen if you continue to feel panicked — such as dying of a heart attack, losing control forever, or ending up in a mental hospital. Your secondary anxiety — your panic about your panic — makes you feel even worse than your first feeling of upsetness; and your obsession with your feelings often prevents you from effectively dealing with them.

If, on the other hand, you view your panic in a paradoxical manner, you may well distract yourself from it, acquire the notion that you can deal with it effectively, and believe that nothing devastating will happen if you continue to experience it. Thus, suppose you tell yourself, and actually believe: "Panic is an exciting state. I'm really alive when I feel it! It shows that I am able to have a wide variety of experiences and I can acquire valuable insights through being panicked."

Thinking this way, you will first of all tend to distract yourself from your feelings of panic. Second, you may actually enjoy them. Third, you will probably stop predicting dire results from experiencing them. Fourth, you may realize that if you can deal with this panic state, you can handle almost any of life's possible Adversities. Paradoxical thoughts and interventions are often startling and shocking, and may jolt you away from awfulizing, and send you back to solving your practical and emotional problems.

Connie was depressed about her failing memory. It would presumably prevent her continuing to teach high school, and cause her to fail graduate courses that gave her salary increases. She also made herself exceptionally depressed about her feelings of depression. Regular REBT methods helped her somewhat — especially convincing herself that she would not be completely boycotted by her principal and by the other teachers if she were less competent than she had previously been. So she moderately improved but kept falling back to feeling depressed.

Connie finally paradoxically used several Zen Buddhist parables, such as thinking of the sound of one hand clapping and focusing on the pleasure of eating a luscious strawberry when she was hanging on a vine from a cliff and about to die. These parables distracted her from her awfulizing. But they also showed her that life could have enjoyments even if she were disapproved, if she never had salary increases, and if she lost her teaching job. The idea that good things could result in the midst of bad happenings seemed at first very paradoxical. But she later realized that this was one of the great paradoxes of life itself and that she could use it to her advantage.

Don't use paradoxical techniques just because they are startling and fascinating, but because you can see that, although they appear at first blush to be wrong, they really have a self-helping goal. Here's an example that we often recommend to our REBT clients: If you are afraid to fail at social encounters, deliberately seek out several rejections by people that you try to befriend. Give yourself the homework assignment, of getting, say, at least three social rejections in one week. If you do this, you probably won't be afraid of getting rejected but may actually welcome it. Not being focused on the "horror" of rejection, you will continue to try and will likely get some acceptances. Moreover, you will be less anxious and may do better in your approaches. You will also, of course, get practice in socializing; and you will see that nothing "awful" happens when you actually are rejected.

This idea of deliberately getting rejected a few times may appear silly, but it is actually designed to help you. You may also devise several other "bad" methods which actually turn out to have good results. Again: pushing yourself to get rejections will at least get you going; thinking about doing some paradoxical things will often let you consider taking risks that you otherwise would not take.

If you have trouble thinking up paradoxical methods that may help you, read some of the literature on this subject, such as the writings of Knight Dunlap, Viktor Frankl, Milton Erickson, and Paul Watzlawick. Talk to your friends about devising suitable techniques. Have a few therapy sessions with a therapist who specializes in paradox. Don't deify paradoxical interventions, but work at them experimentally. Tailor any of them you use to yourself, and abandon them if they do not seem to be working for you.

Using Support Groups, Self-Help Groups, Workshops, and Intensives

Emotive and experiential techniques are often best used with other people, such as in the context of support groups, self-help groups, workshops, and intensives. Fritz Perls, Will Schutz, I, and other therapists have devised a number of experiential exercises that can be effectively employed in these kinds of settings. In support groups, you get together regularly with a number of people who have your kind of problem, openly and honestly discuss your feelings about the problem, find out how others are dealing with it, and sometimes get helpful advice from them. In self-help groups, such as Alcoholics Anonymous (AA), Recovery, Inc., Rational Recovery, and Self-Management And Recovery Training (SMART) groups, you usually get together with other people with problems who help you open up, express your feelings, and accept yourself with your difficulties. In workshops and intensives, the group leaders use a series of experiential and thinking exercises that help you participate and express your honest feelings.

All these groups may be interesting, informative, and helpful. But they also have disadvantages. I advise you not to become a devout follower, or cultist, who unthinkingly follows their ways. Here are some of their disadvantages:

- *Support groups* — such as those in which everyone has cancer or has lost a close relative — may largely consist of people who are not too rational, who are taking their afflictions *too* seriously, and who encourage whining and moaning about their sad fate. If the group you join is largely of this nature, you may find it harmful rather than helpful. You'd be better off to seek out another group or work on your own.
- Some *self-help groups*, like AA groups, insist that your affliction (such as alcoholism) is an incurable disease, that you must attend the group regularly *forever*, and that you absolutely need some kind of Higher Power to help you overcome your troubles. You may actually become addicted to such groups and may give away some of your own powers to heal yourself.
- *Workshops and intensives* are sponsored by leaders who may or may not have your real interests at heart, even when they honestly believe in their own methods. Many of these leaders are not trained professionals and may use highly emotional methods that do

harm as well as good — again diminishing your own powers to help yourself. Many such group leaders are Pollyannaish; and some of them are authoritarian and try to hook you into their cultish practices forever. Some workshops and intensives are money-making devices, and will try to induce you to spend literally thousands of dollars to become "cleared" or "cured." Investigate such groups carefully before you join them. Have a skeptical outlook toward many of their practices. Try not to become obsessively-compulsively hooked on any of them. Use some of their teachings for your own good but don't let yourself become a devout follower. Before you sign up, read Wendy Kaminer's *I'm Dysfunctional, You're Dysfunctional* to see what harm some of these groups may do.

Remember that the essence of much human disturbance is dogma, devoutness, and sacredizing. So see if the groups in which you are interested encourage this kind of disturbed thinking and behavior. If so, think twice — rationally — before seeking their "help."

12

Action Ways to Make Yourself Less Disturbable

When I first became interested in helping myself with my own emotional and behavioral problems, I read a great deal of philosophy and many books on psychology, including the works of pioneering behaviorists Ivan Pavlov and John B. Watson. These writers, along with the leaders of many religious groups, pointed out that *actions speak louder than words* and that if you want to improve your thoughts, feelings, and behaviors, you may have to uncomfortably force yourself to *act differently* than you ordinarily do. By acting against your self-defeating habits, you may become habituated to new and better ways of behaving, become comfortable with and enjoy them, and prove to yourself that you can change in spite of the difficulties of doing so.

So, to overcome my public speaking phobia, and a little later to eradicate my enormous fear of making new social encounters with women, I forced myself to do what I was afraid of and, at the age of 19, almost completely cured myself of both these phobias. By this time in my life I was already immersed in the study of philosophy — especially the philosophy of happiness — and I realized that I was the main creator of my own hang-ups and that I had the power to change my thinking while simultaneously changing my behaviors. So I did both: I convinced myself that it wasn't going to be "terrible," but only highly inconvenient, for me to fail to speak well in public; and I forced myself — very uncomfortably at first — to speak and speak and speak before large audiences in spite of my dread of doing so. I also, a little later, solidly convinced myself that if suitable women refused my overtures for dating, I would be frustrated and deprived, but I wouldn't be a "rotten person," and I wouldn't have to depress myself about their rejections.

As a result of my self-experimentation, and of my gratifying success in overcoming my public speaking and my social phobias, I even wrote a manuscript, when I was in my twenties and had not yet decided to become a therapist: *The Art of Not Making Yourself Unhappy.* I never was able to get this book published, and lost the manuscript when the Institute moved to our new building in 1965. But it contained many of the ideas and practices that I later included in Rational Emotive Behavior Therapy.

How about you? Well, you definitely have the ability, as a human blessed with constructivist tendencies, to think, feel, and behave less disturbedly. As I have said throughout this book — and in all my writings from 1955 onward — you can do this by working on your *thoughts, feelings,* and *actions,* all of which are significantly interrelated. So far in this book I have emphasized *thinking* and *feeling* techniques. Now I shall describe some of the main *action* (behavioral) methods you can use. These won't automatically and permanently change your disturbed thoughts and feelings; but they can darned well help considerably!

Doing What You Are Irrationally Afraid to Do

Many things — such as mountain climbing or criticizing your boss — are truly dangerous or potentially handicapping. You had better have rational, sensible fears of doing them! You stay alive and happy by being cautious, vigilant, and concerned about the poor consequences of some behaviors. You may withdraw, tone down, or modify your possible actions. You look around carefully when crossing the street, and you watch what you are saying to teachers, bosses, and police officers.

Some hesitations and withdrawals, however, are obviously irrational or self-defeating. For example, to refuse to go for job interviews, to avoid speaking up in a group of friends, or to avoid walking the main streets of your city in broad daylight for fear of being shot — these are silly avoidances that get you into trouble or deprive you of real enjoyments. You had better think about them, acknowledge that they may indeed include *some* hazards, but recognize also that refraining them is limiting and probably does you more harm than good.

Okay. But you still may have the habit of withdrawal, blocking yourself in an overly fearful manner. What then?

If you will actively Dispute your Irrational Beliefs about "dangerous" acts, you'll force yourself to do what you are irrationally afraid to do. You can, of course, do so gradually, and minimize the pain of participation. Thus, you can gradually begin to walk on the street, try to date somebody, go for job interviews, or speak up when you are with a group of your friends. The more often and consistently you can do so, the better.

Carl, for example, was afraid of job interviews. He felt that he would do poorly, show his anxiety to his interviewers, always get rejected, and berate himself mercilessly for being anxious and getting rejected. After reading several REBT books, he tried occasional job interviews, but still remained very anxious whenever he had one. As his unemployment insurance began to run out, he feared (rationally) that he'd have to go into his savings in order to live. So he forced himself to go on twenty interviews within a month, even when he thought that he was unqualified for certain jobs and would never get them.

As it happened, none of the interviews worked out, even when he was qualified for the job, although on two occasions he received follow-up calls. In spite of his failures, however, he began to believe strongly what he had previously told himself only lightly: that nothing terrible would happen if he were rejected. He gained excellent experience at being interviewed, and greatly improved his interviewing skills. He even began to enjoy the interviewing process, such as the challenge of giving a good answer when the interviewer was obviously giving him a hard time.

A month later, Carl got one of the jobs he went for. Although it paid less than he wanted to make, he saw that it would temporarily help him financially. For the next few months, while he was on this job, he kept arranging interviews for better jobs and finally got one. He also started to help some of his friends with their job interviewing, showing them how they could use REBT to overcome their anxieties, actually enjoy themselves, and improve their skills.

You can do something similar. Start by identifying which of your actions or inactions are self-defeating and therefore foolish. Are you afraid of several harmless, useful, and enjoyable, pursuits — sports, socializing, walking across bridges, speaking in public? If so, make a list of the disadvantages of your avoidance, and a list of the pleasures of getting over your irrational fears. Use these lists to help convince yourself that, whatever happened to you in these respects in the past — such as speaking in public and being laughed at — was hardly *horrible* or *awful*, however *inconvenient* it may have been. Convince yourself that you did survive failing and will survive it again. See that most failures, if they occur, are harmless. See that your avoidances will make you fear "dangerous" actions more, not less, because you will be telling yourself things like, "If I went in the elevator and it stopped for a few minutes I couldn't stand it! I'd die!"

Show yourself that even though you will at first find it uncomfortable to do what you are avoiding, you can live with the discomfort, handle it, and build up your frustration tolerance about handling it. Recognize that if other people put you down for doing something poorly, that is largely *their* problem. *You* know better than to put *yourself* down for one of your poor *behaviors*. See that your phobia is part of the human condition and that most other people are also unduly afraid of undangerous things, though not necessarily of the ones you are panicked about. Accept yourself with your disability and never damn yourself as a person for having it.

In other words, *get at your Irrational Beliefs (IB's)* that lead you to avoid harmless acts, and strongly and *persistently Dispute these IB's* until you modify or give them up. As you are doing this, make yourself risk — yes, risk — doing what you are terrified of doing, and watch your thoughts and sensations while you are doing it. See how you keep senselessly repeating your IB's, and see how silly they are. Pay close attention to your self-talk and how you needlessly disturb yourself by it. Talk with others, and notice that they have similar IB's. Notice how foolish theirs are, and even help them overcome them, while persisting with Disputing your own.

Take action, action against your phobias and extreme avoidances. Tell yourself that you definitely *can* do so; and keep making yourself do so until your horror diminishes or completely goes away. If you die of doing what you are afraid to do, as we routinely tell our REBT clients, we promise to give you a lovely funeral, with flowers and everything else! You won't die, of course, but you will let a good part of your life die if you *don't* do these "terribly fearful" acts.

Stop doing "easy" things that you deliberately do in order to avoid doing the "frightful" things. For example, you may take long bus rides to work instead of using the "horrible" subway. Or you may tell yourself that you have to stay home and read rather than risk going out socially and being "awfully" rejected. Determine whether some of the things you do are really these kinds of cop-outs. If so, stop yourself from doing them. Or else, as I point out later in this chapter, do pleasant things only *after* you've done some of the things you are afraid to do. Thus, let yourself stay home and read an enjoyable book only *after* you have gone out socially and risked being rejected.

The main thing, again, is to keep risking, risking, risking discomfort until you become comfortable, and then you may actually *enjoy* the previously frightening activity!

The same thing, of course, sometimes goes for trying new experiences: foods and other "dangers." If you are afraid of eating oysters, and force yourself to eat them, you may acquire a real taste for oysters, and enjoy them for the rest of your life. If you are afraid or annoyed about learning to drive a car and you force yourself to learn, you may find that doing so is one of the most enjoyable things that you can do, opening all sorts of new doors in your life.

So again: *Do what you are afraid to do,* and preferably do it often, one time after another. This will not be a total panacea for all your irrational fears. But I'm betting it will be quite helpful!

Using Reinforcement Techniques

Famed psychologist B.F. Skinner, the father of behavior therapy, showed that if you have difficulty doing anything that you know is beneficial, you can stop procrastinating by making yourself do this difficult thing *before* you do an easier or more enjoyable task. Thus, if you must work for an hour a day on a project, but you keep putting it off, you can contract with yourself to do something you really like to do — reading, exercising, talking to your friends — only *after* you have worked on the difficult project for an hour.

Try this technique with the behavioral assignments that you give yourself to help yourself change as you read this book. If you have trouble doing your cognitive homework, going into elevators that you are afraid to enter, or reading the book itself, you can make the assignment more pleasant by doing it only *before* you have done something that you really like to do and that you would feel deprived of if you didn't do. Rewarding yourself in this fashion won't exactly *make* you do the homework that you are avoiding, but it will help push you in that direction, may make the avoided task seem much easier, and will make it more likely that you'll actually *do* it.

You can also assess yourself penalties or punishments when you avoid doing the healthy things that you set yourself to do. Children are sometimes put off by penalties, and often even deliberately do what they are going to be punished for doing. You may act in this same stubborn way; if so, you can see what you are telling yourself to cause your resistance. For instance: "I *shouldn't* be punished for anything that I don't want to spontaneously do. I'll just wait until I *really* feel like doing it. People can't *make me* do anything that I don't like doing! I'll show them!"

This childish resistance is a demand that you must do *only* what you really want to do and must not be forced to do what you dislike — even when, in the long run, it is beneficial for you. You can Dispute your rebelliousness and give it up.

You still may find, however, that you resist doing the hard things that are required to obtain later gains. If so, you can set yourself a punishment for not doing them. Thus, you can make sure that you eat some unpleasant food, spend time with boring people, or do annoying chores (like cleaning the toilet) if you do not do the beneficial things that you have promised yourself to do — for example, exercising, dieting, Disputing your Irrational Beliefs, or overcoming one of your phobias.

It's tough, of course, to actually enact the punishment you set for yourself. Your low frustration tolerance may demand that you *must* not do onerous things, no matter how beneficial they may be. So you may refuse to take a punishment that you set for yourself for not doing difficult tasks. You may have to arrange for friends or relatives to monitor your enacting this punishment when you are delinquent about doing the beneficial tasks that you have set for yourself.

Reinforcing yourself for giving up a serious addiction — say, to alcohol, pot, or smoking — may not work very well because the reward that you use for stopping it may not seem half as pleasurable as the joy you get — at least temporarily! — from your indulgence. But stiff penalties may work if you specifically set them, along with procedures to make sure that you put them into effect, such as having someone close to you enforce your penalties if you refuse to follow them.

Some behavior therapists have suggested the use of extreme penalties. If, for example, you are addicted to drinking every day and you want to stop, you could force yourself to give money to a cause you detest, or burn a hundred-dollar bill, or destroy a book before reading it, every single time that you take a drink. As I often tell my workshop audiences, if you want to quit smoking, you can put the lit end of the cigarette in your mouth every time you take a puff (a punishment), and you can light every single cigarette you smoke with a twenty dollar bill (a penalty). You'll see how long, if you actually do this, you will continue to smoke!

Penalties of these kinds, once again, may have to be monitored by someone else before you actually carry them out. Here's a method, for example, that worked for Jenny, when she had a very hard time stopping herself from smoking pot. Jenny identified a cause she considered obnoxious — the Ku Klux Klan — and wrote a letter to them, saying how much she enjoyed their work and enclosing a hundred dollars in cash. She then gave the letter and the cash to her best friend and roommate, Annabel, with instructions to send it off to the Ku Klux Klan whenever Jenny had a single joint. After Annabel had sent three of these letters with Jenny's money in them and seemed determined to continue this procedure, Jenny stopped smoking pot.

Reinforcements, penalties, and punishments definitely may help you change your dysfunctional behaviors. They do not necessarily, however, help you to change your Irrational Beliefs. Therefore, you're advised to use these methods along with, not instead of, looking for your IBs, actively and vigorously Disputing them, and changing them into healthy preferences.

Using Stimulus Control

When you are addicted to a substance or a behavior, you tend to indulge in it, even though you promise yourself that you won't do so, when certain *stimuli* or *conditions* exist. You will, for example, tend to drink more alcohol at a bar than in a lecture hall and buy more pastry when you pass a bakery than when you do not pass one. You can exert some measure of control over conditions that favor your doing self-defeating things. You can refuse to have cigarettes in your house; stock your refrigerator only with low calorie food; stay away from your drinking and drugging friends; and take a route that avoids the bakery.

Is *stimulus control* an inelegant solution to your indulgence problems? Yes, to some extent it is, because if you allowed yourself to be in tempting situations and *still* resisted them, you would be working harder to overcome your low frustration tolerance (LFT) and would be changing your Irrational Beliefs that create and sustain this LFT. There is no reason, however, why you can't do *both*: Dispute your IB's and *also* employ a measure of stimulus control.

Charles ate too much, including fatty foods, and was warned by his physician about his overweight condition and high blood pressure. He especially liked to go to a good restaurant for lunch with some of his friends and he almost invariably ate too much when he did so, often including a rich dessert. To make himself stop this indulgence, he forced himself to give up most of his outside dining at lunchtime, to bring his own food to work, to eat in the office or in a nearby park, and to avoid good restaurants. As a shame-attacking exercise, he even figured out that he could sometimes go to a fine restaurant with his friends, order only coffee or diet soda, and unwrap the food he had brought along with him, and eat it in the restaurant while his friends were having a regular meal. He got so used to doing this that his initial shame vanished and, while dieting properly, he also lost some of his dire need for others' approval — including that of his friends and the restaurant owner!

Stimulus control, like other REBT methods, can be used by itself, but is better used in conjunction with active Disputing of your Irrational Beliefs and other thinking methods. Although by no means an elegant method of undoing your addictions, it has real utility and may help you in special situations.

Using Time-Out Procedures

You can use *time-out* procedures to good advantage, especially if you combine them with more philosophical methods. "Time-out" means interrupting your disturbed state of mind, emotion, and action to reconsider the course you are on and to give yourself some time to change it. It is especially useful when you are enraged at a friend or intimate and he or she is also enraged at you. Left to your own devices, you will probably call each other names that you don't really mean, take some foolish actions, and escalate your angry reactions. Using a time-out procedure, you agree — preferably beforehand — to take a time-out for twenty minutes or more, separate from each other or maintain a silence together, think things over, and then resume your discussion.

However, you can also take time-out when you get yourself in some kind of trouble while alone. Donald was prone to enrage himself at his neighbors, especially at 2:00 in the morning when they would continue noisy parties, not listen to his pleas over the phone, and even go back to their noise-making after a visit from the police. Naturally, he kept telling himself that they were very unfair, *shouldn't* be that unfair, and *had to* be stopped, so that he could get some sleep and carry on his job as an auditor the next day. He made himself so incensed on these occasions that his blood pressure rose considerably — which he could ill afford — and he did foolish things, including loudly cursing his neighbors and making harassing telephone calls to them for the next few days after the party. He often thought of paying a hit man (or woman) to kill them, but never quite reached that point.

Donald realized that he had better do something to calm himself down, and began to use REBT to discover his violent *musts* about his neighbors and how he could change them back to strong *preferences*. He did fairly well in this respect, but fell back every couple of months or so to intense rage and self-defeating actions. One time, he beat up one of his neighbor's teenage sons, and he came within a hair of going to jail for doing so. On another occasion, the phone company shut off his phone for making harassing calls and he had to do some tall maneuvering to get another phone placed in his apartment.

Donald made a vow that every time he started to feel incensed, he would take time-out for at least 15 minutes, lie down and relax, and do nothing except work at calming himself down before he took any action whatsoever. This worked fairly well, but only temporarily. Soon, or the next day, he was right back fuming and frothing, and sometimes acting foolishly. So he added Disputing to his time-out, and very forcefully began to convince himself that his neighbors *should be* just as unfair and inconsiderate as they were; that he could *stand* their poor behavior; and that he even could enjoy himself, especially by listening to music with ear phones, as long as his neighbors' racket continued. When he began to convince himself of these rational ideas, Donald found that he remained much less angry for longer periods of time, and that, when his neighbors started one of their raucous parties again, he mainly felt very annoyed and irritated at their actions but was not furiously damning nor determined to stop them at all costs.

Time-out, then, can be quite useful in its own right, but you can use it more effectively if you see how you are creating the disruptive feelings that you are trying to get away from and if you work on changing your basic demands that are largely creating these feelings.

The Use of Skill Training

REBT, like other effective psychotherapies, tries to help you stop seriously upsetting yourself about almost anything obnoxious that occurs in your life. But, as I noted in the section on problem solving in Chapter 9, it also tries to help you solve your practical problems. Difficulties often arise because you may lack skills in certain areas, such as sports, dancing, socializing, and job hunting. Once you calm yourself down about your inadequacies in these areas, you can add pleasure and competency to your life by getting skill training.

In your interpersonal relations, one of the most useful skills is undemanding and unangry assertion. On the one hand, you may be too non-assertive or passive, because you are afraid that if you ask for the things you want you will be refused, and that will "prove" that you are a worthless individual or "show" that you can get virtually nothing you really want. In this respect, you have a dire *need* for acceptance, or you think you *absolutely must* have your wishes granted. You can tackle these problems — which are really emotional problems — by finding your irrational musts and minimizing them. But you still may lack some of the skills required for effective assertiveness.

On the other hand, you may demand that other people do your bidding and you may assert yourself in a raucous, angry manner — which often turns people off and encourages them to give you less of what you want. Here, once more, you usually have the grandiose demand that people *absolutely must* give you your "due" and that they are *no good* when they don't. If so, look for your internal and external commands, change them to preferences, and make yourself assertive rather than aggressive.

Once you work on the philosophy of wanting but not needing, and on desiring but not insisting that people stop bothering you to do things you don't want to do, you can learn specific skills of assertion. A good therapist, a series of effective workshops, or suitable books and cassettes can be used to help you acquire these skills. Then, of course, you had better practice actually using them.

You can also acquire other skills in therapy, in courses, in workshops, and by written and recorded materials. Many skills — such as playing the piano or becoming adept at tennis — will give you greater life enjoyments. Some of them — like communication and social skills — will help you get along better at work and at play. Of course, you don't *have to* become a great expert at anything, but if you are deficient in any skills that you find important, you can get some training in them. First, however, stop putting yourself down for lacking such skills. The more you put yourself down for being deficient in assertion, conversation, or other skills, the more you may block your proficiency and participation in them.

Which brings us back to the two emotional problems that are usually so important: self-downing and low frustration tolerance (LFT). If you especially use REBT to acquire unconditional self-acceptance (USA) when you are skill-deficient and to acquire high frustration tolerance (HFT) about going through the difficulties of skill-training, you will be more able to learn the skills that you desire.

And that can lead directly to greater happiness and remarkably less disturbability.

13

Onward to Self-Actualization and Increased Happiness

Most psychotherapies have at least two main goals: First, helping people to reduce their disturbances; and second, encouraging them to increase their happiness and self-fulfillment. Rational Emotive Behavior Therapy has always specifically tried to help people in these two ways. In our original edition of *A Guide to Rational Living* in 1961, Robert Harper and I showed our readers how to relieve their problems — and how to acquire what we called "a vital absorbing interest" and other means of achieving self-actualization.

Attempt to make yourself vitally absorbed in some persons or things outside yourself. You are born and reared with a strong tendency to love and to want to be loved. Other people often beautifully interact with you, because you and they are social creatures. Children, adolescents, and most adults naturally love and want return love. Even in non-romantic cultures, we tend to fall "madly" in love with at least a few people during our lifetimes. And most of us love our family members, mates, and close friends unromantically. Why? Because it is part of our nature to love others.

Attachment to things, objects, projects, and causes has its great rewards, and may well enhance your life. You can, for example, vitally absorb yourself in playing a sport, in practicing a profession, or in building a business or a political organization. This kind of absorption may sometimes be more durable and more involving than loving other people. Ideally, you can love both persons and things. But if you impel yourself, especially for a period of time, into a vital absorbing interest, you may achieve what psychologist M. Csikszentmihalyi calls "flow," and you may greatly enjoy yourself.

If you look for an absorbing interest, try to find persons or activities in which you can honestly absorb yourself for your own sake. It may look fine and noble if you devote yourself to your family members, to a social cause, or to one of the helping professions. But you have a right, as a human with your own personal tastes, to devote yourself "selfishly" to an avocation — such as coin collecting or restoring antique cars — that has relatively little "social" value. If you are happy doing so, you may even become a better citizen and less sabotaging of your social group.

Commit yourself to a challenging, long-range, rather than a simple and short-range, project. You may quickly master simpler endeavors, such as checkers, and then find them boring. To write a comprehensive history of checkers will engage you a lot longer! So you may find it best to choose a long-range goal, such as writing novels, making scientific discoveries, or becoming a busy entrepreneur.

Incidentally, it is lovely to *succeed* at your chosen field of interest but don't think that you absolutely *have to* do so. Get rid of your musts and you will find that your involvement itself is fascinating, even without notable success.

Also, you don't have to discover an absorbing field spontaneously. You may have to look around for something vital, push yourself experimentally into a chosen field, and persist at it for a while before you become really absorbed in it. Don't abandon a project until you give it an honest, fairly long try. Then, if you still don't thrill to it, look around, experiment some more, and choose a different commitment. Nor do you have to stick to a single vital absorbing interest all your life. You may relish one for a few years, then replace it with another, and another, and still another — if you live that long!

Even if you have a major endeavor, you may decide to vary your interests and to enhance some side projects. A varying of your hobbies, your circle of friends, and your other involvements may help you remain more zestful than if you stay in one major routine.

Bob Harper and I saw psychotherapy as enhancing happiness as well as alleviating disturbance in the late 1950s, and we still do. Self-actualization has been enthusiastically endorsed over the years by Abraham Maslow and many other social thinkers, including Rudolf Dreikurs, S.I. Hayakawa, Carl Jung, Alfred Korzybski, Rollo May, Carl Rogers, Ted Crawford, and others. It is an important concept in humanistic and existential psychology.

Does this mean that to lead a good life you *absolutely must* have a long-term, involving interest? No! You are different from other people, and what's good for you may not be good for them. Individuals, in fact, are so varied that some can be healthy and happy living as beachcombers. Not too many, perhaps. But some!

You don't easily achieve self-actualization when you are disturbed. You tend to be overwhelmed with anxious and depressed feelings, leaving little energy to pursue desirable goals. Moreover, your goals themselves may be destructive — such as a dire need to succeed at almost anything. Having such a "necessity" can be a vital absorbing interest that keeps you busy all your life. But not too happily! In fact, you may indulge in self-defeating behaviors because you feel driven to do so, to hook yourself on obsessions, compulsions, and panic states, to avoid experiencing unoccupied or dull moments. Disturbance can be truly exciting! So you may not be motivated to give it up — and thereafter lead a less thrilling existence!

But is it worth it? Rarely! Will destructive pleasures enable you to look for bigger and better enjoyments, and to work for achieving them? Not very well! They are often so involving that they hardly give you the time or energy to think about making yourself happier. Your disturbances can easily block you from achieving self-fulfilling goals.

The Limitations of Self-Actualization

Does self-actualization have limitations? Indeed it does. Many critics, such as Maurice Friedman, Martin Buber, Christopher Lasch, and Brewster Smith, point out that Abe Maslow's version of self-actualization is too individualistic and non-social — that it largely ignores the fact that humans are social creatures and that if they mainly seek *self*-fulfillment they may sabotage some of their best *group* interests. Adlerian therapists, who emphasize social interest, certainly do not push narcissism.

Kenneth Gergen, James Hillman, Edward Sampson, and other commentators have also noted that self-actualization is largely a Western concept. Some Asian and other cultures stress sociality and put the group above the individual members. Other critics of self-actualization have also shown that because it includes goal-seeking, as you seek for progress, you also discover more about it and change it. This goes along with the REBT idea that you had better view self-fulfillment in an experimental, changing way.

Don't forget that even when you mainly strive for social, rather than individual goals, you are still making a personal *choice* to do this; and in this sense you are still individualistic and self-deciding. Also, the survival of the human race involves *both* individualistic and social goals. Unless each of us personally strives to stay alive and be happy, and also to help others, the human race might well die out.

You have the right, as a unique person, to choose to seek self-actualization. If you do so, you may consider trying to achieve the goals described in the following section, which most psychotherapists, including those following REBT, endorse. Give these suggestions serious thought — but I suggest that you not rigidly choose any of them. These goals can help you to achieve mental health, to make yourself less disturbable, and to enhance your enjoyment and happiness.

Potential Goals for Self-Actualization

Nonconformity and individuality. You can try to be an individual in your own right — to be "your own person." You can dovetail this goal with the goal of living cooperatively in your social group and trying to preserve social well-being. Instead of an *either/or* view, take an *and/also* attitude that includes social *and* individual interest. As you strive for sensible individuality and freedom of choice in sex, love, marital, vocational, and recreational realms, don't insist that your way is the only "right" way; encourage others to take *their* chosen pathways.

Social interest and ethical trust. As just noted, to be self-actualizing you had better be importantly devoted both to your own goals and values and, simultaneously, accept the fact that you are a member of the social system. With pure self-interest you may harm your group, and possibly sabotage the whole human race. Strive to do what you really want to do, *but also* to be a good model for others, to help individual others, and to live so as to generally benefit humanity.

Self-awareness. To become well-functioning and less disturbed, you will be aware of your own feelings and unashamed of having them. You will acknowledge both your positive and your negative feelings, but not necessarily act on the latter. You will — for the most part — keep your panic and rage to yourself! And you'll do your best to reduce them. You will strive to change yourself — and often the environment as well. As S. I. Hayakawa put it, "know yourself," but also realize how little you know about yourself and keep trying to discover what you "really" want and do not want.

Acceptance of ambiguity and uncertainty. To be self-actualizing is to accept ambiguity, uncertainty, and some amount of disorder in your life and in the world. As I noted in 1983, "Emotionally mature individuals accept the fact, that, as far as has yet been discovered, we live in a world of probability and chance, where there are not, nor probably ever will be, absolute necessities nor complete certainties. Living in such a world is not only tolerable, but in terms of adventure, learning, and striving, can even be exciting and pleasurable."

Tolerance. Be open-minded. Respond to similarities and differences, rather than ignoring differences among things that have the same name. You do not see all trees as green, all education as good, or all modern art as silly. Emotionally sound people are intellectually flexible, tend to be open to change, and are prone to take an unbigoted view of the infinitely varied people, ideas, and things in the world around them.

Commitment and intrinsic enjoyment. As Bob Harper and I noted in *A Guide to Rational Living*, if you are self-actualizing, you tend to enjoy pursuits (e.g., work) and recreations (e.g., golf) as ends or pleasures *in themselves*, not mainly as *means* towards ends (e.g., working for money or playing golf to achieve good health). You tend to commit yourself to long-term vital absorbing interests, rather than only to brief pleasures.

Creativity and originality. Abraham Maslow, Carl Rogers, S. I. Hayakawa, Rollo May, and other writers show that persons who are more fully functioning are often, though not necessarily, creative, innovative, and original. Because you do not direly need others' approval nor bow down to conformity, you tend to be more self-directed than other-directed, more flexible than rigid, and to look for original solutions to issues and problems that you *personally* favor, instead of for what you "*should*" go along with.

Self-direction. When you are emotionally healthy and enjoying, you will tend to be true to yourself as well as to others. While interdependent with others and at times asking support from them, you will largely plan and plot your own destiny (within, of course, a social context). You will not overwhelmingly need outside support to "make sure" that you do the "right thing."

Flexibility and scientific outlook. Science not only uses empiricism and logic to check its hypothesis, but it is also intrinsically open-minded, undogmatic, and flexible — as Ludwig Wittgenstein, Bertrand Russell, Karl Popper, W. W. Bartley, Gregory Bateson, and other philosophers of science have shown. REBT emphasizes that you largely upset yourself with rigid, imperative shoulds and musts. But you have the ability to make yourself less disturbed and more self-actualizing when you question and challenge necessitizing and prefer alternative-seeking.

Unconditional acceptance of yourself and others. Paul Tillich, Carl Rogers, and other social thinkers have emphasized the value of people unconditionally accepting themselves and others. From its start, REBT has done this, too; and Michael Bernard, Paul Hauck, Janet Wolfe, David Mills, Tom Miller, Russell Grieger, Philip Tate, Paul Woods, I, and a number of other REBT authors have said that you can undo much of your disturbances and be self-actualizing if you will learn to evaluate your thoughts, feelings, and actions — in regard to your goals and purposes — while refusing to globally rate your "self," your "essence," or your "being." REBT also encourages you to accept others unconditionally and unbigotedly, while still evaluating their thoughts, feelings, and actions.

Risk-taking and experimenting. Self-actualizing usually goes along with a good degree of risk-taking and experimenting. Try many tasks, preferences, and projects in order to discover what you personally want and do not want. Keep risking possible defeats and failures if you want to achieve maximum involvement in life.

Long-range hedonism. Hedonism — the philosophy of seeking pleasure and avoiding pain and frustration — seems necessary to human survival and fulfillment. Short-range hedonism — "Eat, drink, and be merry for tomorrow you may die!" — has its good points and its limitations. For tomorrow you may well be alive with a hangover! Or dead with a heart ailment! To more fully actualize yourself, strive for intensive and extensive pleasure today *and* tomorrow.

All of the above goals reveal my own prejudices, as well as those of most practitioners of REBT, because they constitute our view of what is probably better for you to do to reduce your disturbances and to increase your potential for and realization of greater happiness. Other therapists often agree with many of these aims, and some research has shown that when people strive for them they get better results, although a great deal more scientific investigation of these goals and values is needed.

Think about self-actualization and consider experimenting in your own life along the above lines. All these methods may have real disadvantages, especially if you take them to extremes. It's all too easy to overdo it, to try frantically to get what you really want in life, to neglect other people, to be hated by them, and to harm the social group in which you live. In the long run, you may thereby defeat yourself.

Another danger: If you push self-actualization too hard and define it as winning others' approval, you may wind up devoting yourself to what "they" want you to do rather than what *you* truly would like to do. This is what happens when people join cults, such as those run by Jim Jones, Bagwan Rashneesh, Luc Jouret, and Shoko Asahara (the leader of the Japanese Aum Shinrikyo cult). If you let yourself be hooked into a sect such as one of these, you may unassertively follow your Leader's or Guru's goals and interests. Not too self-actualizing! And potentially life-threatening.

So push your way into self-fulfillment, if you will, but take care to realize exactly what is truly actualizing *for you.* The best watchwords would seem to be: experimenting, risk-taking, and adventuring. By all means try to make yourself emotionally healthier, happier, and more fulfilled. These goals usually overlap considerably. But evaluate your chosen goals carefully, and be ready to retreat when you obtain doubtful or harmful results.

A final word on self-actualization: musturbation about self-fulfillment is not very self-fulfilling. Attempting to be *fully* or *perfectly* self-actualized can be self-sabotaging! Extremism, even in this good area, may bring dubious results.

14

Some Conclusions on Making Yourself Happy and Less Disturbable

Let me sum up with some ideas you can think about. I've made three main points in this book:

One: *You largely bring on your own emotional disturbances by choosing, both consciously and unconsciously, to think irrationally, to create unhealthy negative feelings, and to act in self-defeating ways.* Fortunately, therefore, you can *choose* to change your thinking, feelings, and behaviors to undisturb yourself. If you do so in a forceful, persistent manner, by using several of the main techniques of Rational Emotive Behavior Therapy (REBT), you can make yourself considerably less disturbed — that is, less anxious, depressed, enraged, self-hating, and self-pitying — and sometimes do so in a short period of time. Follow the methods described in this book and keep practicing them. They aren't magical or miraculous. But they definitely can help!

Two: *If you use REBT techniques regularly whenever you think, feel, and act self-defeatingly you can make yourself remarkably less disturbable.* You may then only rarely upset yourself — and may ward off emotional difficulties when you are about to experience them.

Three: *If you give yourself the specific goal of making yourself less disturbable, and if you use some of the methods outlined in Chapters 7 and 8, you will give yourself a much better chance to achieve this goal.* Be purposive and pushy about achieving less disturbability!

Back to the major objective — as shown in Chapter 7 — building your will power to change your *actions*. Be determined, get the knowledge to back your determination, and act on your determination and your knowledge.

As emphasized throughout this book, you are a complex *thinking, feeling,* and *acting* person; and REBT therefore gives you many growth methods. Obviously, however, your thoughts or philosophies are a crucial aspect of your self-changing. For even when you work hard to modify your feelings and your behaviors, you have to *think* about doing so, *plan* to do so, and keep *plotting* and *scheming* to change.

All personality change seems to have many crucial cognitive elements. (Psychotherapists and counselors may wish to read more about this in my book for professionals: *Better, Deeper, and More Enduring Brief Therapy*.) Here's a summary:

- First, you'd better be fully *aware* of the possibility of your changing.
- Second, you had better *choose* a goal, *decide* to pursue this goal, *determine* to carry it out, and *push yourself* to implement it.
- Then, while working at changing, you will *assess* your progress, *decide* how to continue (or not continue), *observe* whether you are succeeding, *plan* new possible moves, *push yourself* to carry out your plans, *observe* your new results, *reflect* on whether you are reaching your goals, *revise* some of your goals, plans, behaviors, and continue the cycle.
- You also will *consider, choose, review, experimentally try,* and *evaluate* the methods you employ to help you change. Working on your feelings and your behaviors (as well as on your thoughts) involves numerous cognitive (thinking) processes and cannot merely be done in, of, or by itself. Thinking elements always seem to be — and strongly seem to be — involved when you effect any personal change; and when you make deep and intensive changes, some reflection is crucial.

To take the road to making yourself less disturbable, you had better make some deep *philosophical* changes. You may sometimes be able to dispense with the thinking steps — or at least you may *think* you can! If you join a religious or political group, for example, you may suddenly feel and act much differently than you did before. But, really, such changes occur because you *decided* to adopt the ideas of the group you choose and to work at following them. If you almost die by drowning or by a disease, you may make yourself into a "new person," but, again, you obviously *decide* to make this change, *think* about adopting it, and *push yourself* to adopt your new ways.

Rather than do this kind of thinking sloppily, without much conscious awareness, why not *consciously* figure out where you want to go and precisely how to get there? Making yourself less disturbable is surely one of the most important things you can do. Why not follow some of the suggestions in this book and *use your head* to get there?

Can You Make Yourself Less Disturbable On Your Own?

No controlled experiments have yet demonstrated the exact path you can take to make yourself less disturbed. As I noted in Chapter 6, many experiments have shown that psychotherapy clients, and particularly those who are treated with REBT and Cognitive-Behavior Therapy (CBT), distinctly improve, and often in a period of only a few months. In a few of those studies it has also been demonstrated that clients achieve lasting improvement, two years or more after their therapy has ended. But, as mentioned, research studies have not yet fully shown how clients become distinctly less disturb*able.*

Assuming that you can make yourself less disturbable, can you actually do so on your own? My answer is Yes — because I have talked with hundreds of people who have seemed to achieve it. Many were treated by me and/or by other REBT practitioners, but some had little or no psychotherapy and made unusual progress by reading and listening to REBT materials and working on their own. Most of these individuals were diagnosed as everyday neurotics, but a number had severe personality disorders, and a few were even diagnosed as psychotic and had spent some time in mental hospitals.

I have been convinced that these people were definitely less disturbable than before they used REBT materials. In some instances, they even suffered unusual setbacks — such as long-term unemployment, bankruptcy, or serious accidents and diseases — after they improved. But they were able to weather these life storms without upsetting themselves. Naturally, we'd better view their stories of great emotional improvement with some degree of skepticism. I still support their progress, however, and look forward to controlled experimentation that will provide more convincing evidence in regard to these self-helpers.

My correspondence with thousands of readers of *A Guide to Rational Living* has particularly convinced me that a large number of them, with and without psychotherapy, have made notable improvements in their lives through reading. A smaller but still sizable number have helped themselves to become significantly less disturbable, and their success is impressive.

Acknowledging my own prejudices, my talks and correspondence with thousands of people over the years have made me enthusiastic about the results that many people have achieved with self-help materials — including books by Robert Alberti and Michael Emmons, Aaron Beck, Michael Broder, David Burns, Gary Emery, Windy Dryden, Arthur Freeman, Paul Hauck, Paul Woods, and a number of other leading REBT and CBT authors. For, as I have written, and as a number of other researchers — such as J. T. Pardeck and S. Starker — have also pointed out, self-help materials offer their readers and listeners several advantages. Here are a few of them:

- Many people with emotional problems actually learn more by reading than they do by working with therapists or with self-help groups.
- Others who get little out of reading find that they help themselves considerably with audio and video aids.
- A large percentage of people in therapy can deepen their improvement by simultaneously using self-help materials.
- Many individuals have not the time, money, or desire for psychotherapy, and therefore have little choice but to use written and recorded aids, and they often benefit considerably by using them.
- People have ended their therapy sessions and prevented themselves from falling back to their disturbances by the use of home study materials.
- People who feel that it is shameful or disgraceful to attend actual therapy sessions and who, for wrong reasons, fail to do so, are able to benefit from self-help materials.
- People who do not have regular therapy but who attend self-help groups like Alcoholics Anonymous, Recovery, Inc., Rational Recovery, Self-Management And Recovery Training (SMART), and Women For Sobriety groups often improve with self-help books and tapes.

This does not mean that the use of self-help materials has no disadvantages. It often does. For instance:

- Users of these materials are not accurately diagnosed, may treat themselves for disorders — such as attention deficit disorder, or multiple personality disorder — that they do not actually have, and may suffer harm in doing so.
- Many self-help products are mainly designed to make money or to enhance the reputation of their authors, and include material that is unhelpful and even harmful.
- Some materials — especially some of the New Age items — discourage their users from going for psychotherapy which they could well benefit from and encourage them to join, instead, sects and crackpot organizations that do more harm than good.
- Self-help materials offer the same messages to all readers and listeners, and if these are indiscriminately followed they may well help some individuals but contribute to the harm of others.
- These materials are rarely tested by controlled experiment, to determine whether they are effective with the populations that use them. Publishers of the materials are far more interested, usually, in getting them out fast and making a quick profit on them than they are in discovering whether or not the materials have real therapeutic value.

For reasons such as these, you had better be skeptical about many self-help materials and procedures, especially those that are heavily advertised. Test them out, use them with some degree of caution, and see if they are actually helpful to you. Discuss them, if you can, with professionals and with other individuals who have used them. Seriously consider them as an adjunct to psychotherapy, and/or with courses and workshops led by professionals. (My suggestions for suitable REBT and CBT self-help materials are starred entries in the Reference section at the back of this book.)

Realistic Expectations of "Cure"

Can anyone, including you, totally cure himself or herself of what we usually call *emotional disturbance*? Most probably not.

You, like the rest of the people in the world, seem to have a strong tendency to make yourself easily disturbable. You don't have to do this to yourself, but you often do. You have, as I keep emphasizing in this book, the native ability to *solve* practical and emotional problems, and to *change* your thoughts, feelings, and actions when you behave foolishly and self-defeatingly. You can often do this remarkably well, and make yourself considerably less disturbable than you have been.

But not *completely* unruffled. If you could accomplish this, you would rid yourself of even your *healthy* negative feelings — sadness, regret, frustration, annoyance — when unfortunate Activating Events occur. How would you then survive? Not very well!

Even if we talk about ridding yourself entirely of unhealthy, self-sabotaging feelings — such as panic, depression, and self-hatred — what are your chances? Exceptionally slim. You would then have to quickly, automatically and always react sensibly and sanely to life's Adversities. Always? Perfectly? Fat chance!

Again: You would never slip or fall back to disturbance. You would, for example, enrage yourself against one of your relatives or coworkers, realize they were fallible humans who acted badly (but were hardly totally rotten people), forgive the sinner but not the sin, quickly make yourself displeased with their *actions*, but refuse to damn *them*. Good. But would you never, never, never, when they treated you or others unfairly, fall back to feeling enraged again? Hardly.

So you definitely can make yourself less disturbable, if you work hard at using some of the methods in this book. But not completely undisturbable. Not while you are still a fallible human. If you teach your relatives, friends, coworkers, and associates some of the main REBT methods, you may be able to help them become less disturbed and make themselves less prone to future disturbance. Not always, of course, but sometimes.

Other individuals, including perhaps you, have additional limitations. Some people, for example, are mentally limited, with more than usual difficulties thinking straight and doing regular problem solving. A few are severely retarded and unable to take care of themselves. Many of these individuals can, with considerable training, improve and function better. But only, as I briefly noted in Chapter 2, within limits.

A good many people also have limited emotional functioning. A few are psychotic — perhaps schizophrenic or manic. A larger number have severe personality disorders, and sometimes have psychotic episodes but can still take care of themselves and sometimes achieve remarkably well. These include individuals with severe depression, obsessive-compulsive disorders, psychopathic outbursts, schizoid behavior, borderline personality disorder, and other personality disorders.

The REBT theory holds that most individuals with *serious* personality disorders are born with some biological deficits. They have innate tendencies, often increased by environmental difficulties, to be deficient in important thinking, emotional, and behavioral respects. Intellectually, they may have over-focusing or under-focusing deficiencies. Emotionally, they may easily over-react or under-react. Behaviorally, they may be overly impulsive or compulsive. Frequently, the neurotransmitters in their brains, such as serotonin, do not function normally and they may have various other kinds of biochemical malfunctioning. If you suffer from a personality disorder, you may be diagnosed and helped with medication — such as Prozac or Xanax.

If you or one of your close associates has a severe personality disorder, can effective psychotherapy really help? Definitely. People with severe personality disorders, in fact, had better have some amount — and often a considerable amount — of psychotherapy, as well as possible medication. Many of them only function well in their personal and vocational lives with this kind of treatment.

How about self-help procedures? People with severe personality disorders, though hardly completely cured, are often enormously benefited by self-help groups and support groups, by religious and social groups, and by self-help materials. Alcoholics Anonymous, Recovery Inc., and Self-Management and Recovery Training (SMART), often help them considerably; and literally millions of people function better with help from effective self-help pamphlets, books, audio and video cassettes, and other materials. Many, indeed, who for one reason or another do benefit from psychotherapy also help themselves through various self-help channels.

So if you or any of your relatives, friends, or associates are more seriously disturbed, by all means try psychotherapy, medication, self-help groups, and other forms of treatment. Experiment. Investigate. Persist. Find whatever help you can, and work hard at using it. If at once you don't succeed, try, try again! Get a proper diagnosis. Acknowledge what your particular disorder is, and accept yourself unconditionally with it. Under guidance from your doctor, experiment, perhaps, with medication, until you find what works for you. Get intensive psychotherapy — with which you can also experiment. Don't give up. Don't say that you *can't* change. Just admit that you find it difficult.

Can you try for the elegant solution that I advocate in this book — to make yourself less disturbed and less disturbable? Yes, by all means. You probably will have to try harder and longer to achieve it than if you were less disturbed, persistently and forcefully counteracting your innate tendencies, breaking your habitual patterns of over-reacting or under-reacting, and changing your Irrational Beliefs about your natural handicaps. For that is what constitutes a severe personality disorder: First, tendencies to have thinking, emotional, and behavioral deficits. Second, Irrational Beliefs or cognitive distortions about these handicaps.

You can see how this is the case. Suppose, for example, someone has a physical disability: a cleft palate, a crippled limb, congenital deafness. People with such conditions function worse than those who are not disabled. Moreover, they are often criticized, laughed at, and put down as persons for being disabled. Many of them, of course, savagely criticize their *selves*, and not merely their *performances*. They add to their physical disabilities by making themselves disturbed *about* their disabilities. And it gets worse: their emotional problems add to their physical problems and almost always make them more disabled.

People with severe personality disorders often have similar dismal experiences. They tend to know that they have certain intellectual, emotional, and behavioral deficiencies, and they deplore having them. They also tend to know that they have more frustrations than other people have — that their lives really *are* more difficult. They know, in many instances, that others often discriminate against them and put them down for having "defects." Consequently, they (like the rest of the human race) almost always are disturbed *about* their personality disorder. First, they defame themselves for being deficient. Second, they horrify themselves about their unusual difficulties and develop low frustration tolerance about them. Third, they may blame others, thrive on being victims, and block their chances to change.

Vernon had a severe case of OCD — obsessive-compulsive disorder. He checked almost every important (and often unimportant) decision that he made twenty or more times! If he had to turn off a light, lock his car, or shut off a faucet, he did so many times before he was really satisfied that he had done so properly. He consumed so much time going through this checking process — which he often realized was foolish and nonproductive but "couldn't" force himself to stop — that even though he was quite bright and could have finished college, he had to leave school with an Associate Arts degree and accept a clerical position.

Vernon hated himself for his "idiotic" checking, and he ranted and raved that his life was "too hard" and that it *absolutely should not* be that handicapping. So he spent large amounts of time berating himself and whining about his disability. His self-deprecation and low frustration tolerance created severe feelings of depression, so that he wound up being much more handicapped than he otherwise would have been had he suffered from OCD alone. He lived in Wyoming and was never able to come to New York to work with me face-to-face, but he arranged to have a number of telephone sessions and to read practically all my self-help books.

After twenty sessions of telephone psychotherapy on a twice-a-month basis, and occasional sessions thereafter, Vernon began to thoroughly accept himself with his seriously handicapping OCD. At first, he became more *in*tolerant of having this handicap, and ranted about the "enormous unfairness" of being afflicted. But after seeing that his low frustration tolerance was just about as disabling as his obsessive-compulsive disorder, he worked hard against it and made himself *exceptionally sorry and disappointed*, but not *awfulizing*, about his disability. He took it as a challenge to overcome rather than as a "horror" to rant about. By the time our regular sessions ended, Vernon was much more self-accepting than most of my clients and had a high degree of frustration tolerance. He then used this tolerance to work very hard on cutting down his compulsive checking, and got to the point where he only checked two or three times rather than 20 or more times, and thereby saved himself about two hours every day. He decided to return to college and become a computer specialist, and was able to enjoy life considerably more.

Could Vernon have achieved the same result without psychotherapy and merely by using REBT self-help materials? Of course, we'll never know. But clients with his severe disturbance usually would have required more than the twenty phone sessions that he had. He suggested that we end these steady sessions, and only have additional ones every once in a while, because he was doing so well with REBT books and audiovisual materials. Since we stopped the regular sessions three years ago, he has only had six additional phone sessions with me, and has continued to make distinct gains using self-help materials.

Other people, too — some of whom have only corresponded with me or seen me briefly at the talks and workshops I give in various parts of the world — have had no therapy sessions, have only used REBT self-help procedures, and have said that they appreciably improved their severe personality disorders. Naturally, some of them may have exaggerated their conditions and/or their gains. But I am convinced that many severely disturbed individuals can appreciably benefit from self-help materials; some seem to achieve profound philosophical changes and to make themselves distinctly less disturbable.

Maintaining and Enhancing Your Self-Therapy Gains

In 1984 I wrote an article on how REBT clients can maintain and enhance their therapy gains. The Albert Ellis Institute in New York publishes the paper, and it has helped many clients. Here are some of the main points in that article that you can use in your own self-therapy.

How to Maintain Your Improvement

When you improve by using REBT, but and you fall back again to old feelings of anxiety, depression, or self-downing, try to pinpoint exactly what thoughts, feelings, and behaviors you once changed to bring about your original improvement. If you have again made yourself feel depressed, think back to how you previously used REBT to reduce your depression.

For example, you may remember that you stopped telling yourself that you were worthless when you failed at work or at love and that you stopped saying that a poor slob like you couldn't ever succeed in life. You may have forced yourself to go on job interviews or to try to date suitable partners and thereby showed yourself that you could do so, even though you may have been anxious at that time. You may have used Rational Emotive Imagery to imagine of one of the worst things that could happen to you, let yourself feel very depressed about this, and then worked at making yourself feel healthily sorry and disappointed, instead of feeling unhealthy feelings of depression. Remind yourself of thoughts, feelings, and behaviors that you have changed and that you have helped yourself by changing.

Keep thinking and rethinking Rational Beliefs (RB's) or coping statements, such as: "It's great to succeed but I can fully accept myself as a person and enjoy life considerably even when I fail!" Don't merely parrot these statements but go over them carefully many times and *think them through* until you really begin to believe them and are helped by believing them.

Keep discovering and Disputing the Irrational Beliefs (IB's) with which you are once again upsetting yourself and Dispute them realistically: "Is it true that I *have* to succeed in order to accept myself as a worthwhile, deserving person?" Dispute them logically: "Does it follow that if I fail at an important task I will *always* fail at it?" Dispute them practically: "Where will it get me if I believe that I *absolutely must not* be frustrated or rejected?"

Keep forcefully and persistently Disputing your IB's whenever you see that you are letting them creep back again. Even when you don't actively hold them, realize that you may underlyingly still believe them, bring them to your consciousness, and preventively — and vigorously! — Dispute them.

Keep risking and doing things that you irrationally fear — such as riding in elevators, socializing, job hunting, or creative writing. Once you have partly overcome one of your self-defeating fears, keep acting against it regularly. If you feel uncomfortable when you force yourself to do things that you unrealistically fear doing, don't sink back to avoidance — and thereby preserve your discomfort forever! Often, make yourself as *un*comfortable as you can be, in order to work on your low frustration tolerance and to make yourself truly, lastingly comfortable — and often able to enjoy the feared situation(s) — later.

Try to see clearly the difference between having *healthy* negative feelings when Adversities occur — such as sorrow, regret, and frustration — and bringing on *unhealthy* negative feelings about the same Adversities — such as panic, depression, and self-hatred. When you experience disturbed feelings, assume that you have created them with some dogmatic *shoulds, oughts,* or *musts.* Find these demands, and change them back to *preferences.* Don't give up until, by using Rational Emotive Imagery or other REBT methods, you actually change your disturbed emotions to healthy negative feelings.

Avoid self-defeating procrastination. Do unpleasant but useful tasks first and fast — today! If you still procrastinate, reward yourself with enjoyable things — such as eating, reading, or socializing — only *after* you have performed the tasks that you are avoiding. If you then still procrastinate, give yourself a severe punishment or penalty — such as talking to a boring person for an hour or burning a hundred-dollar bill (pick a value that will *hurt!*) — every time that you foolishly delay.

Show yourself that you can make an absorbing *challenge* and a real *adventure* of maintaining your emotional health and keeping yourself reasonably happy *no matter what misfortunes* you experience. Make the uprooting of your misery one of the most important aspects of your life — something you are utterly determined to steadily work at achieving.

Remember — and keep using — the three, main Insights of REBT:

Insight No.1: You mainly feel the way you think and therefore *you largely can control how you feel* when faced with Adversities.

Insight No.2: Although you mainly adopted and created self-sabotaging Beliefs and habits in the past, you now, in the present, consciously and unconsciously maintain them — and that is why you are *now* disturbed. Your past history and your present life conditions importantly affect you, and so do your innate predispositions. But your present philosophy, which you keep actively reaffirming, is the *main* contributor to your current disturbances.

Insight No.3: There is *no magical way to change* your personality and your strong tendencies to needlessly upset yourself. Only through work and practice — yes, *work* and *practice* — are you likely to change your irrational Beliefs, your unhealthy feelings, and your self-destructive behaviors.

Steadily — and unfrantically! — look for personal pleasures and harmless enjoyments. Try to devise for yourself an intense, long-range vital absorbing interest. Take as a major life goal the achievement of emotional health and of real enjoyment. Try to be a long-range rather than a short-range hedonist.

Keep in touch with several other people who know REBT and who can help you remember and review some of its aspects. Tell them about your problems, show them how you are using REBT to cope with them, and see if they agree with your solutions and if they can suggest additional and better kinds of answers.

Practice teaching REBT to some of your friends and relatives who are willing to let you try to help them with it. The more often you use it with others, clearly see their Irrational Beliefs and self-destructive behaviors, and try to help them change, the more you will tend to understand the main REBT principles and to use them yourself. When you see other people act destructively, try to figure out — with or without talking to them about it — what their main IB's probably are and how these can be actively and vigorously Disputed.

Keep reading REBT writings and listening to and watching suitable audio and video cassettes. Use them to remind yourself about and to keep working at some of the main REBT philosophies and actions.

How to Deal With Your Backsliding

Accept your backsliding, if it occurs, as normal. Accept it as something that happens to almost all people who first improve emotionally and who then fall back to disturbed thoughts, feelings, and behaviors. See it as part of your human fallibility. Don't put yourself down and bring on destructive feelings of shame and hopelessness if your old symptoms return. Don't think that you have to handle them entirely by yourself and that it is wrong or weak for you to seek some sessions of therapy and to talk to your friends about your problems.

When you backslide, try to see clearly that your *behavior* is unfortunate but you are never a *bad or rotten individual* because of it. At these times, particularly go back to the important REBT principle that you had better only rate the effectiveness of what you think, feel, and do, and never rate *yourself*, your *being*, your *essence*, or your *totality*. No matter how badly you fall back, work at achieving unconditional self-acceptance (USA). Fully accept yourself with your weak and foolish behavior — and then keep trying to change this behavior.

Go back to the ABC'S of REBT and look again for your Irrational Beliefs at point B: for your absolutistic *shoulds, oughts*, and *musts*; for your *awfulizing* and *terribilizing*; for your *damning* of yourself and other people; and for your overgeneralizing *always* and *nevers*. As noted above, persistently and vigorously Dispute all your main IB's until you strongly believe Effective New Philosophies (E's) that will point the way to once again reducing your disturbances.

Keep looking for, finding, and forcefully Disputing your IB's. Do this, over and over, until you build intellectual and emotional muscle (just as you would build physical muscle by exercising and continuing to exercise).

Don't merely parrot rational coping self-statements or Effective New Philosophies. Test how *strongly* you actually believe these healthy ideas. Challenge your weak Rational Beliefs and make them stronger. Challenge your Rational Beliefs (RB's), to see that you truly can maintain them in the face of questioning. Use a number of REBT's emotive techniques — such as saying coping statements to yourself very powerfully — to help you vigorously believe your helpful philosophies. Don't rest with lightly believing, but work at strongly convincing yourself of the usefulness of your Rational Beliefs. Convincing yourself lightly or "intellectually" of your new Effective Philosophies is nice but won't help very much or persist very long. Do so strongly and vigorously, do so many times, and check to see how you truly believe them.

How to Generalize About Your Disturbances and About Alleviating Them

When you are mainly working to relieve one set of your emotional problems — such as your terror of public speaking or of being rejected in your personal relationships — try to see how these significantly overlap with other problems, as well as with many of the disturbances of other people. Thus, as noted in Chapter 3, your anxieties about both public speaking and personal rejection include (1) your Beliefs that you *absolutely must not* fail and be disapproved; (2) that doing so would be *awful* and *horrible*; (3) that you *can't stand* or *bear* the horrendous frustration involved in such failures; (4) that you would be a *worthless person* if you failed and were disapproved of; (5) that your failing once or a few times in these important respects would mean that you would *always* fail and *never* be respected; and sometimes (6) that failing really doesn't matter *at all* and you couldn't care less.

If you see these similarities in virtually all your disturbances (and those of other people), you can understand how to approach and to reduce almost any of your other severe anxieties (or depressions or rage). Fascinating — and very useful — knowledge!

If therefore, you overcome your horror of speaking badly in public, you can use your knowledge of how you overcame it to reduce your horror of being rejected in your social or love relationships. And if you subsequently develop some new terror — say, of losing your job or of being the worst tennis player in your neighborhood — you can fairly easily see how to deal with that "terror" too. For your Irrational Beliefs, disturbed feelings, and self-defeating actions are part of your *general* repertoire of thoughts, feelings, and actions that you bring to different kinds of Adversities. Once you use REBT effectively in one set of conditions, you can realize that in just about all cases in which you upset yourself you are sneaking in one or more of your common IB's. Consequently, if you reduce them in one area and then find you are emotionally disturbed in another respect, you can use the same REBT principles and practices to discover and change your IB's in the next area.

This is why REBT can help you to become happier and less disturbable. By using it you can show yourself that it is difficult to remain disturbed in *any* way if you change your basic IB's. If you decrease your absolutistic, dogmatic *shoulds, oughts*, and *musts*, and if you replace them with flexible, alternative-seeking (though often still strong) *desires* and *preferences*, you will rarely disturb yourself in the first place and will quickly be able to undisturb yourself even if you carelessly slip back into unhealthy ways.

Let me not be too optimistic here. I am not contending that if you consistently use REBT you will automatically overcome all your emotional disturbances and soon get yourself to a point where you will always be happy and never seriously upset yourself again. It's not that easy or automatic. But I am saying that if you learn the general principles of REBT and undisturb yourself in one important area, and if you really try to use them in other areas, you will see that they are generally applicable.

Better yet: You will tend to see that there really are no absolutistic, unconditional musts in the universe, and that devoutly believing in any of them will lead to needless disturbance. You will realize that many Adversities are deplorable but that none of them, except by your arbitrary definition, are really *awful, horrible*, or *terrible*. You will acknowledge that whatever bad things happen to you, you can almost always stand them, survive them, and be reasonably happy in some ways in spite of them. You will habituate yourself to see that when you and other people act in damnable *ways*, you and they are not damnable, bad, and undeserving *persons*. You will still effectively use generalizing but will not overgeneralize and "see" that one failure leads to *always* failing and that a few rejections do not mean that you will *never* be accepted by important others in your life.

I formulated REBT's general philosophy in the 1950s to help myself and my clients notably reduce our powerful tendencies to needlessly disturb and upset ourselves over Adversities. A great amount of clinical and experimental evidence since that time shows that REBT, along with the methods of several of the other cognitive-behavior therapies, actually provides much relief from emotional pain. But what I did not clearly see in the early days of REBT, and what I now increasingly realize, is that consistent use of its philosophical system also helps many people to be much less disturbable than they were before. And that's a happy discovery!

Would you like to be one of these happier, less disturbable people? Try strong and persistent REBT and see for yourself!

Rational Chicken Soup for Your Head and Your Heart

If you work at using the theories and practices described in this book, you can keep convincing yourself of a number of profound philosophies that will most likely help you do three things:

1. *To reduce your present disturbed thoughts, feelings, and actions.*

2. *To make yourself distinctly less disturbable — less prone to new and future disturbances.*

3. *To actualize yourself more fully, to create greater life enjoyments, and to live happier.*

To achieve these goals here are some realistic, hard-headed, and practical self-statements — "Rational Chicken Soup" — that you can think about, modify, and work at carrying out:

- Although it is often *highly preferable* for me to perform well and win the approval of others, and thereby to achieve my main goals and purposes, I never *have* to do so.
- No matter what "bad" things — against my strong interests and desires — happen to me (or I *make* happen) they are *only* bad, they never, except by my foolish definition, are so bad that they *absolutely must not* occur. When they do occur, they are not *awful* — meaning *totally* bad or "badder than they *should* be."
- Even when the worst things happen, I can practically always *stand it*, still remain alive, and still, again, find *some* happiness in living, if I strongly convince myself that I can!
- I may often think, feel, and act foolishly, stupidly, and neurotically but I never, never *am* a *fool*, a *worm*, or a *rotten*,

damnable person. I never *am* what I *do* — even if I wrongly think I am!

- I therefore can strongly refuse to evaluate or rate my *self*, my *being*, my *essence*, or my *personhood*, but can and will only rate my *acts, deeds*, and *performances*. Cross my heart and hope to live!

- I will also only rate other people's acts, feelings, and thoughts and refuse to rate — and especially refuse to damn — their *self, being*, or *essence*. They often *act* wormily, but they *are* not worms!

- I will also only rate the *conditions* under which I live, in regard to how they fulfill my and my social group's goals and interests. But I will not globally rate *the world* or *life* as "good" or "bad." The *world* never stinks — only some of its *aspects*.

- I can and will use and increase my will power or ability to change my thoughts, feelings, and behaviors by making an effort to clearly *decide* to change; by *being determined* to act on my decision; by *acquiring relevant knowledge* of how best to act; by *forcing myself to act* even when I find it uncomfortable to do so. My "will power" that includes *no action* also includes *no power*.

- If I am determined to work at making myself less disturbed and less disturbable, and if I actually keep working at this problem, I can most probably do so. But I cannot be super-human, perfect, or totally undisturbable. Not as long as I am a fallible human!

- What I want to do I shall try to do. I will not assume that I *can't* do most things without first trying to do them. I will try many difficult things to *see* if I can or cannot accomplish them.

- What I truly can't do, I simply can't. Tough!

- I shall usually try to avoid extremism — to refuse to see things as *all* good or *all* bad. I shall try to avoid extreme optimism and extreme pessimism. A more balanced, more realistic approach will be my usual goal. But even that goal I shall not take to extremes!

- My past solutions to my emotional problems were great! Now how can I improve them?

- I'll never be totally undisturbable — unless I'm dead. Now how can I make myself *less* disturbable — while I'm still alive?!

- I really have some great assets, along with my flaws and liabilities. But that doesn't make *me* great. Now let me *enjoy* my assets! And let me use my intellectual assets to accept myself when I could use more assets!
- I can try to gain insight into the origins and history of my disturbances, but I prefer to gain insight into what I am now doing to maintain them and what I can now do to change them. I want *insight* into how to *outlaw* my disturbances!
- I like *knowing* that I am competent and efficient at important projects. But that doesn't make me a *competent individual* or a *good person.* Nothing does! I will strive to be skillful because of the enjoyment and good results I get. Not to prove that *I* am okay!
- Feeling ashamed of what I do helps correct my foolish behavior. Feeling ashamed of me, the doer, "helps" me to avoid correcting it and unduly restricting my life.
- If the Martians get down here, and they're sane, they will die laughing at how a bright person like me can often act so foolishly. I'd better learn to laugh with them.
- The bad things that happen to me — or that I *make* happen — are rarely *all* bad. I can usually find some advantages in them — and learn from their drawbacks. I can especially enjoy the *challenge* of refusing to unduly upset myself about them.
- Avoiding doing what I am irrationally afraid to do will help me avoid overcoming my fears and phobias. Risking is far less risky!
- I am concerned about my health, about getting into accidents, and about dangerous activities, and I take proper precautions to prevent harm to myself and my loved ones. But I cannot control the universe, so I rarely worry about unusual dangers occurring. My worry does not stop the tides!
- When I have a hard or boring task to do procrastination will not make it easier. I try to procrastinate about procrastinating!
- Denying that I have emotional problems denies my solving them. Rationalizing about them is hardly rational!
- I like to assert myself and express my real feelings. But it is often best to keep my big mouth shut with bosses, professors, and traffic cops!
- People are often much different from me and from each other. And they damned well *should* be!

- I enjoy convincing others of my point of view. But I can accept disagreements without being disagreeable. I rarely consider suicide when I lose an argument.
- I hate to be treated shabbily or unfairly but I don't *have to* be treated well and *need not* dwell on it or be vindictive when I am not. Obsessing about injustice is an injustice to myself.
- No matter how important I make being loved by a specific person, I realize that there are other important people that I can love and be loved by. Yes, some!
- I often like the company of others but can be quite happy when I am completely alone. I can often be my own best friend!
- I will do my best to enjoy several things and not to addict myself to one kind of thinking, feeling, or acting. I will have some revulsion for compulsion!
- I will probably actualize *my disturbances* and not *myself* unless I work at making myself less disturbed and less dis-turb*able*.
- By achieving and maintaining a vital absorbing interest, I increase my chances of attaining experiences of *flow* — that is, enjoying what I am doing for its *own* sake, not necessarily for other rewards, and not to prove what a *good person* I am. I flow with my flow because *I* find it intrinsically interesting and enjoyable. If it helps me and others in additional ways, too, that's gravy!
- Science is not sacred but has its great values for myself and others. When I adopt goals and purposes, I can strive to achieve a scientific outlook that favors continual hypothesiz-ing, testing, and checking; that tentatively accepts social and material "reality"; and that works for human (and nonhu-man) betterment.
- Achieving full, complete, or total self-actualization — or almost anything else! — is impractical and idealistic. More actualization, yes. Full and complete, no. Let me not be unrealistically greedy!
- As with self-actualization, so, again, with disturbability. Complete undisturbability is superhuman. I am a fallible human. No human, as far as we know, is superhuman. Q.E.D. — which was to be proved!

Selected References

The following references include the works of the main authors mentioned in this book, as well as an additional number of items on Rational Emotive Behavior Therapy (REBT) and Cognitive Behavior Therapy (CBT), which may be useful for self-help purposes. The self-help materials are preceded by an asterisk (*) and many of them are obtainable from the Albert Ellis Institute, 45 East 65th Street, New York, NY 10021-6593. The Institute's free catalog and other materials for distribution may be ordered on weekdays by phone (212-535-0822), by fax (212-249-3582) or e-mail (orders@rebt.org). The Institute will continue to make available these and other materials, and it will offer talks, workshops, and training sessions, as well as other presentations in the area of human growth and healthy living and list these in its free regular catalog. Some of the references listed, especially a number of self-help materials, are not referred to in the text.

Alberti, R., & Emmons, M. (1995). *Your perfect right*, 7th ed., San Luis Obispo, CA: Impact Publishers, Inc.

*Adler, A. (1927). *Understanding human nature*. Garden City, NY:Greenberg.

Bandura, A. (1997). *Self-efficacy: The exercise of control*. New York: Freeman.

*Barlow, D. H., & Craske, M. G. (1989). *Mastery of your anxiety and panic*. Albany, NY: Center for Stress and Anxiety Disorders.

Bartley, W. W., III. (1984). *The retreat to commitment*, rev. ed. Peru, IL: Open Court.

Bateson, G. (1979). *Mind and nature: A necessary unit*. New York: Dutton.

*Beck, A. T. (1988). *Love is not enough*. New York: Harper & Row.

*Benson, H. (1975). *The relaxation response*. New York: Morrow.

*Bernard, M. E. (1993). *Staying rational in an irrational world.* New York: Carol Publishing.

*Bernard, M. E., & Wolfe, J. L., (Eds.). (1993). *The RET resource book for practitioners.* New York: Institute for Rational-Emotive Therapy.

*Broder, M. S. (1990). *The art of living.* New York: Avon.

Buber, M. (1984). *I and thou.* New York: Scribner.

*Budman, S. H., & Gurman, A. S. (1988). *Theory and practice of brief therapy.* New York: Guilford.

*Burns, D. D. (1989). *Feeling good handbook.* New York: Morrow.

Carnegie, D. (1940). *How to win friends and influence people.* New York: Pocket Books.

*Coué, E. (1923). *My method.* New York: Doubleday, Page.

*Crawford, T. (1993). *Changing a frog into a prince or princess.* Santa Barbara, CA: Author.

*Crawford, T., & Ellis, A. (1989). A dictionary of rational-emotive feelings and behaviors. *Journal of Rational-Emotive and Cognitive-Behavioral Therapy, 7*(1), 3-27.

*Csikszentmihalyi, M. (1990). *Flow: The psychology of optimal experience.* San Francisco: Harper Perennial.

DeShazer, S. (1985). *Keys to solution in brief therapy.* New York: Norton.

Dewey, J. (1929). *Quest for certainty.* New York: Putnam.

*Dreikurs, R. (1974). *Psychodynamics, psychotherapy and counseling.* Rev. Ed. Chicago: Alfred Adler Institute.

*Dryden, W. (1994c). *Overcoming guilt!* London: Sheldon.

*Dryden, W. (Ed.). (1995). *Rational emotive behaviour therapy: A reader.* London: Sage.

*Dryden, W., & DiGiuseppe, R. (1990). *A primer on rational-emotive therapy.* Champaign, IL: Research Press.

*Dryden, W. & Gordon, J. (1991). *Think your way to happiness.* London: Sheldon Press.

*Dunlap, K. (1932). *Habits: Their making and unmaking.* New York: Liveright.

*Ellis, A. (1957a). *How to live with a neurotic: At home and at work.* New York: Crown, Rev. ed., Hollywood, CA: Wilshire Books, 1975.

*Ellis, A. (1962). *Reason and emotion in psychotherapy.* Secaucus, NJ: Citadel.

*Ellis, A. (1972). Helping people get better rather than merely feel better. *Rational Living, 7*(2), 2-9.

*Ellis, A. (Speaker). (1973). *How to stubbornly refuse to be ashamed of anything.* Cassette recording. New York: Albert Ellis Institute.

*Ellis, A. (Speaker). (1974). *Rational living in an irrational world.* Cassette recording. New York: Albert Ellis Institute.

*Ellis, A. (1976a). The biological basis of human irrationality. *Journal of Individual Psychology, 32,* 145-168. Reprinted: New York: Albert Ellis Institute.

*Ellis, A. (Speaker). (1976b). *Conquering low frustration tolerance.* Cassette recording. New York: Albert Ellis Institute.

*Ellis, A. (Speaker). (1977c).*Conquering the dire need for love.* Cassette recording. New York: Albert Ellis Institute.

*Ellis, A (Speaker). (1977d). *A garland of rational humorous songs.* Cassette recording and songbook. New York: Albert Ellis Institute.

*Ellis, A. (1985). *Overcoming resistance: Rational-emotive therapy with difficult clients.* New York: Springer.

*Ellis, A. (1988). *How to stubbornly refuse to make yourself miserable about anything—yes, anything!* Secaucus, NJ: Lyle Stuart.

Ellis, A. (1994a). *Rational emotive imagery.* Rev. ed. New York: Albert Ellis Institute.

*Ellis, A. (1994b). *Reason and emotion in psychotherapy.* Revised and updated. New York: Birch Lane Press.

Ellis, A. (1996). *Better, Deeper, and More Enduring Brief Therapy.* New York: Brunner/Mazel.

Ellis, A. (1996). *How to maintain and enhance your rational emotive behavior therapy gains.* Rev. ed. New York: Albert Ellis Institute.

Ellis, A. (1998). *How to control your anxiety before it controls you.* Secaucus, NJ: Carol Publishing Group.

*Ellis, A., & Becker, I. (1982). *A guide to personal happiness.* North Hollywood, CA: Wilshire Books.

*Ellis, A. & Blau, S. (1998). (Eds.). *The Albert Ellis Reader.* Secaucus, NJ: Carol Publishing Group.

*Ellis, A., & Dryden, W. (1990). *The essential Albert Ellis.* New York: Springer.

Ellis, A., & Dryden, W. (1997). *The practice of rational emotive behavior therapy.* New York: Springer.

Ellis, A., Gordon, J., Neenan, M., & Palmer, S. (1998). *Stress counseling.* New York: Springer.

Ellis, A., & Harper, R. A. (1997). *A guide to rational living.* North Hollywood, CA: Wilshire Books.

*Ellis, A., & Knaus, W. (1977). *Overcoming procrastination.* New York: New American Library.

*Ellis, A., & Lange, A. (1994). *How to keep people from pushing your buttons.* New York: Carol Publishing Group.

Ellis, A., & MacLaren, C. (1998). *Rational emotive behavior therapy: A therapist's guide.* San Luis Obispo, CA: Impact Publishers.

*Ellis, A., & Tafrate, R. C. (1997). *How to control your anger before it controls you.* Secaucus, NJ: Birch Lane Press.

*Ellis, A., & Velten, E. (1992). *When AA doesn't work for you: Rational steps for quitting alcohol.* New York: Barricade Books.

*Ellis, A., & Velten, E. (1998). *Optimal aging: Get over getting older.* Chicago: Open Court Publishing.

Emery, G. (1982). *Own your own life.* New York: New American Library.

Erickson, M. H. (1980). *Collected papers.* New York: Irvington.

*FitzMaurice, K. E. (1997). *Attitude is all you need.* Omaha, NE: Palm Tree Publishers.

*Frank, J. D., & Frank, J. B. (1991). *Persuasion and healing*. Baltimore, MD: Johns Hopkins University Press.

*Frankl, V. (1959). *Man's search for meaning*. New York: Pocket Books.

*Franklin, R. (1993). *Overcoming the myth of self-worth*. Appleton, WI: Focus Press.

*Freeman, A., & DeWolfe, R. (1993). *The ten dumbest mistakes smart people make and how to avoid them*. New York: Harper Perennial.

Freud, S. (1965). *Standard edition of the complete psychological works of Sigmund Freud*. New York: Basic Books.

*Fried, R. (1993). *The psychology and physiology of breathing*. New York: Plenum.

Friedman, M. (1976). Aiming at the self: The paradox of encounter and the human potential movement. *Journal of Humanistic Psychology, 16*(2), 5-34.

Froggatt, W. (1993). *Rational self-analysis*. Melbourne: Harper & Collins.

Gergen, R. J. (1991). *The saturated self*. New York: Basic Books.

*Glasser, W. (1999). *Choice theory*. New York: Harper Perennial.

Goleman, D. (1995). *Emotional intelligence*. New York: Bantam.

*Grieger, R. M. (1988). From a linear to a contextual model of the ABCs of RET. In W. Dryden and P. Trower, eds. *Developments in cognitive psychotherapy* (pp. 71-105). London: Sage.

*Hauck, P. A. (1991). *Overcoming the rating game: Beyond self-love— beyond self-esteem*. Louisville, KY: Westminster/John Knox.

Hayakawa, S. I. (1968). The fully functioning personality. In S. I. Hayakawa, (Ed.), *Symbol, status, personality* (pp. 51-69). New York: Harcourt Brace Jovanovich.

Hill, N. (1950). *Think and grow rich*. North Hollywood, CA: Wilshire Books.

Hillman, J. (1992). One hundred years of solitude, or can the soul ever get out of analysis? In J.K. Zeig (Ed.), *The evolution of psychotherapy: The Second Conference* (pp.313-325). New York: Brunner/Mazel.

Hoffer, E. (1951). *The true believer*. New York: Harper & Row.

Horney, K. (1950). *Neurosis and human growth*. New York: Norton.

Jacobson, E. (1938). *You must relax*. New York: McGraw-Hill.

*Johnson, W.R. (1981). *So desperate the fight*. New York: Institute for Rational-Emotive Therapy.

Johnson, W.B. (1996, August 10). Applying REBT to religious clients. Paper presented at the Annual Convention of The American Psychological Association, Toronto.

Jung, C. G. (1954). *The practice of psychotherapy*. New York: Pantheon.

Kaminer, W. (1993). *I'm dysfunctional, you're dysfunctional*. New York: Vintage.

Kelly, G. (1955). *The psychology of personal constructs*. New York: Norton.

Klee, M., & Ellis, A. (1998). The interface between rational emotive behavior therapy (REBT) and Zen. *Journal of Rational-Emotive & Cognitive-Behavior Therapy, 16*, 5-44.

Korzybski, A. (1933). *Science and sanity.* San Francisco: International Society of General Semantics.

Lasch, C. (1978). *The culture of narcissism.* New York: Norton.

*Lazarus, A. A., & Lazarus, C. N. (1997). *The 60-second shrink.* San Luis Obispo: Impact.

*Lazarus, A. A, Lazarus, C., & Fay, A. (1993). *Don't believe it for a minute: Forty toxic ideas that are driving you crazy.* San Luis Obispo, CA: Impact Publishers.

*Low, A. A. (1952). *Mental health through will training.* Boston: Christopher.

*Lyons, L. C., & Woods, P. J. (1991). The efficacy of rational-emotive therapy: A quantitative review of the outcome research. *Clinical Psychology Review, 11,* 357-369.

Mahoney, M. J. (1991). *Human change processes.* New York: Basic Books.

Maltz, M. (1960). *Psycho-cybernetics.* Englewood Cliffs, NJ: Prentice-Hall.

Maslow, A. (1968). *Toward a psychology of being.* New York: Van Nostrand Reinhold.

*Maultsby, M.C., Jr. (1984). *Rational behavior therapy.* Englewood Cliffs, NJ: Prentice-Hall.

May, R. (1969). *Love and will.* New York: Norton.

*McGovern, T. E., & Silverman, M. S. (1984). A review of outcome studies of rational-emotive therapy from 1977 to 1982. *Journal of Rational-Emotive Therapy, 2*(1), 7-18.

Meichenbaum, D. (1997). The evolution of a cognitive-behavior therapist. In J.K. Zeig (Ed.), The evolution of psychotherapy: The Third Conference (pp. 95-106). New York: Brunner/Mazel.

*Miller, T. (1986). *The unfair advantage.* Manlius, NY: Horsesense, Inc.

*Mills, D. (1993). *Overcoming self-esteem.* New York: Albert Ellis Institute.

Moreno, J. L. (1990). *The essential J. L. Moreno.* New York: Springer.

Niebuhr, R. See Pietsch, W.V.

Nielsen, S.L. (1996, August 10). Religiously oriented REBT. Examples and dose effects. Paper presented at the Annual Convention of the American Psychological Association, Toronto.

Pardeck, J. T. (1991). Using books in clinical practice. *Psychotherapy in Private Practice, 9*(3), 105-199.

Pavlov, I. P. (1927). *Conditional reflexes.* New York: Liveright.

Perls, F. (1969). *Gestalt therapy verbatim.* New York: Delta.

Piaget, J. (1954). *The construction of reality in the child.* New York: Basic Books.

*Pietsch, W.V. (1993). *The serentiy prayer.* San Francisco: Harper San Francisco.

Popper, K. R. (1985). *Popper selections.* Ed. by David Miller. Princeton, NJ: University Press.

Rank, O. (1945). *Will therapy and truth and reality.* New York: Knopf.

Rogers, C. R. (1961). *On becoming a person.* Boston: Houghton-Mifflin.
*Russell, B. (1950). *The conquest of happiness.* New York: New American Library.
Russell, B. (1965). *The basic writings of Bertrand Russell.* New York: Simon & Schuster.
Sampson, E. E. (1989) The challenge of social change in psychology. Globalization and psychology's theory of the person. *American Psychologist, 44,* 914-921.
Schutz, W. (1967). *Joy.* New York: Grove.
*Schwartz, R. (1993). The idea of balance and integrative psychotherapy. *Journal of Psychotherapy Integration, 3,* 159-181.
*Seligman, M. E. P. (1991). *Learned optimism.* New York: Knopf.
*Silverman, M. S., McCarthy, M., & McGovern, T. (1992). A review of outcome studies of rational-emotive therapy from 1982-1989. *Journal of Rational-Emotive and Cognitive-Behavior Therapy, 10*(3), 111-186.
*Simon, J. L. (1993). *Good mood.* LaSalle, IL: Open Court.
Skinner, B. F. (1971). *Beyond freedom and dignity.* New York: Knopf.
Smith, M. B. (1973). On self-actualization. *Journal of Humanistic Psychology, 13*(2), 17-33.
*Spivack, G., Platt, J., & Shure, M. (1976). *The problem-solving approach to adjustment.* San Francisco: Jossey-Bass.
*Starker, S. (1988b). Psychologists and self-help books. *American Journal of Psychotherapy, 43,* 448-455.
*Tate, P. (1997). *Alcohol: How to give it up and be glad you did.* 2nd. ed. Tucson, AZ: See Sharp Press.
Taylor, S. E. (1990). *Positive illusions: Creative self-deception and the healthy mind.* New York: Basic Books.
Tillich, P. (1983). *The courage to be.* Cambridge: Harvard University Press.
*Vernon, A. (1989). *Thinking, feeling, behaving: An emotional education curriculum for children.* Champaign, IL: Research Press.
*Walen, S., DiGiuseppe, R., & Dryden, W. (1992). *A practitioner's guide to rational-emotive therapy.* New York: Oxford University Press.
*Warren, R., & Zgourides, G. D. (1991). *Anxiety disorders: A rational-emotive perspective.* Des Moines, IA: Longwood Division Allyn & Bacon.
Watson, J. B. (1919). *Psychology from the standpoint of a behaviorist.* Philadelphia: Lippincott.
Watzlawick, P. (1978). *The language of change.* New York: Basic Books.
Wittgenstein, L. (1922). *Tractaeus logico-philosophicus.* London: Kegan Paul.
*Wolfe, J. L. (1992). *What to do when he has a headache.* New York: Hyperion.
*Woods, P. J. (1990a). *Controlling your smoking: A comprehensive set of strategies for smoking reduction.* Roanoke, VA: Scholars' Press.
*Young, H. S. (1974). *A rational counseling primer.* New York: Albert Ellis Institute.

About the Author

Dr. Albert Ellis is the author of more than sixty-five books on psychotherapy and relationship therapy, including *Reason and Emotion in Psychotherapy, A Guide to Rational Living, Better, Deeper, and More Enduring Brief Therapy, How to Control Your Anxiety Before it Controls You, Rational Emotive Behavior Therapy: A Therapist's Guide*, and *The Albert Ellis Reader*.

Dr. Ellis has been rated by his peers in the United States as the second most influential psychologist (Carl Rogers came first and Sigmund Freud third) and by his peers in Canada as number one in importance. He has revolutionized American psychotherapy since 1955, when he created Rational Emotive Behavior Therapy (REBT), the first of the now popular cognitive behavior therapies.

Dr. Ellis is president of the Albert Ellis Institute in New York City, where he sees a large number of individual and group therapy clients, leads its psychotherapy training program, conducts research activities, and gives numerous talks and workshops every year. He also is a very traveled speaker who gives many professional talks and workshops throughout the world.

Index

—MORE BOOKS WITH *IMPACT* —

Please see the following page for more books.